Road Trip!

Chasing Blue Skies on Roads That Go Forever

Ross S. Robbins

ISBN: 0615771971
ISBN-13: 9780615771977

Cover Photo: Ann Robbins

DEDICATION

To my loving wife Ann; My favorite road trip partner and frequent co-conspirator, my reserve when I get weary, my watcher-over when I get frazzled and my best reason for going places. The first question I asked as we started dating: "Do you like Road Trips?"

She answered "Yes!"

CONTENTS

ACKNOWLEDGMENTS

No adventure of any kind can begin without lots of support. From the friends who accompanied me on these trips, Ann Robbins, The LOUTS (Brian Green, Geoff Cole and Rod Thonger), and my long time car pals Jim Hegy, John Kurowski and others. I am also deeply indebted to my logistical supporters like Bill Roushey and Roy Pogue Thank you all.

I also am indebted to all the mechanical support from Tom Beauchamp, Ben Wofford, all the above names and many more. None of this would have happened without all of you.

Oh, and thanks to Google Maps and Rand McNally. You are the greatest time wasters I know other than the trips themselves.

Road Trip!

1 INTRODUCTION

You may wonder how it is that I was motivated to take all the trips that resulted in this collection of short stories. On the other hand you may not care at all. Still I feel compelled to give you some insight into the logic or illogic that generated all these adventures. The best way to explain it is to use another story to illustrate the thought process. This story is not mine.

In the wonderful 1978 John Landis movie "Animal House", The Delta House has just been kicked off campus by Dean Wormer after violating "Double Secret Probation". Boon (Peter Riegert) and Larry (Tom Hulce) one of the pledges to Delta House, are approaching the house as movers are confiscating all the contents including a life sized mermaid and an actual cow, only to see Bluto (John Belushi) grumbling and kicking a little yellow Crosley. Hoover (James Widdoes) the house president and the only close to responsible person in the entire fraternity, stands by helplessly.

The scene plays like this:

BOON: *Geeez. What's going on?*
HOOVER: *They confiscated everything...even the stuff we didn't steal.*
BLUTO: *They took the bar! The whole f**king bar!*

Otter (Tim Matheson) drives up in his Corvette observing this scene, casually grabs a full bottle of Jack Daniels from a movers box and wings it to Bluto who drinks it down without pause or stopping for air.

BLUTO: *Thanks. I needed that.*

BOON: *Christ. Otter, this is ridiculous.*

LARRY, in despair: *What are we going to do?*

OTTER AND BOON, simultaneously: **Road Trip!**

This is the spirit that launched most of the adventures in this book. It also accurately depicts the typically thorough thought process that precedes a departure. There is nothing so liberating yet useless as a Road Trip. A Road Trip is one with no purpose other than the going. If one is moving to a new job or going off to college or to a new home, it is not a Road Trip; it has a purpose. In order to be a real Road Trip, the trip itself must be the purpose…and, just to be clear, driving an old car home after buying it, rather than shipping it, cannot be construed as a purpose - rather it is a clear choice. It is a choice to make a Road Trip.

Welcome to some of my favorite Road Trips!

2 MY TOY CAR DISEASE

While this is not a Road Trip story, and certainly no way to start a book with that title, I thought it would be useful to put the cars in some sort of context. Here is how they fit into the arc of the experiences I have had with all the cars that passed through my hands.

After raising my kids to the point where they were eating their own food and not cleaning their own rooms, I thought it was time for a sports car.

I found an Austin Healey 3000 in 1984 to fill that item on my bucket list. After driving this lovely lorry for eight years it was time for the next item on the bucket list…racing! But race what? I had driven a Lotus Elan that was for sale when out in California on business in 1991. I drove it through the hills of the east bay near Danville and it was fantastic. I thought about it for racing but while this Elan was a lovely road car, the cost of converting it to a vintage eligible car was going to be pretty high not to mention spelling the ruin of a good road Elan. So instead I acquired an Austin Healey Sprite with a full vintage race specification and ticked the racing box.

For two years I campaigned that Sprite and learned race craft and car control. One of my most favorite photos shows the inside front wheel about six inches off the ground at Topeka, just like Jim Clark in a Cortina. But the Sprite wasn't fast enough without me overstressing it and I kept breaking axles. After two years I needed more speed capability. Based on track success I saw, the fabled Lotus marque was first on my list as I looked for a faster car.

A long time vintage racer called Harry Mathews had advertised a race prepared Lotus Seven that was in my price range if I sold everything but my kidneys so I went for a look. For whatever reason, I simply couldn't fit in that car. Harry had his mechanic remount the race seat as far back as possible and take out a side bolster but still "Lardo" couldn't fit.

Maybe I would if I removed my kidneys? As I was about to give up and look elsewhere, Harry suggested that his race prepped Elan might just be available - at a price about fifty percent higher than the Seven. However, I demurred, thinking that I really do need my kidneys.

The ever resourceful Harry offered an easy financing plan (Buy Here, Pay Here!!) and I was hooked. Since the Elan was almost exactly the same size and weight as the Sprite, I wouldn't need a bigger trailer or tow vehicle and storage would be similar, so justifying the purchase was easy. All I had to do was sell the big Healey *and* the Sprite and I was into the Elan nice and clean. Done and Done.

In October 1994 I owned my first Lotus. Red with yellow bumpers and numbers, it still had a full interior with carpet and vinyl as well as a beautiful wood dash. On the other hand it had but one racing seat and a dry-sumped engine rated at about 160 bhp. I was in heaven. Not only was it prettier than the Sprite it was faster. A lot faster. Now I was the owner of a nicely prepared, excellent condition, right hand drive Elan that had been successfully raced by Harry's family and, other than an image, I had absolutely no idea what I had. When I went to pick it up, I even had to figure out how to tie it down on my trailer while not hurting the fiberglass body, and that is no easy thing. But we managed, this little charmer and me, getting more and more comfortable with the relationship. If you remember the girls on Gilligan's Island, the Sprite was like Mary Ann while the Elan was like Ginger.

My first race at Second Creek raceway in Denver was a dating disaster. I kept spinning the car on the entrance to turns at the end of both major straights. What had I done? I should have stayed with Mary Ann! It seems the speed I was carrying in the Elan was substantially more than that in the Sprite and therefore my braking point couldn't be the same despite the better brakes. I know that seems obvious in retrospect, but the Elan was so comfortable in handling, size and input that it simply went faster with no more effort. Finally, I learned where to brake and thus began a 15 year love affair. After a full rebuild in 2000, she was even better, just about perfect in every way.

My little redhead and I travelled countrywide to the racetracks I had only read about. We didn't get them all but got most of the majors in the western 2/3 of the country. From Pacific Raceways in Washington, Portland International in Oregon and Sears Point and Laguna Seca in California, we set respectable lap times and top five finishes in class all along the west coast. Along with all the Colorado tracks, Mid-Ohio,

Road America, Topeka, and Texas World were some of the Midwest tracks we played on with much the same result. After a couple of long hauls we ticked the boxes on Mosport, Virginia International Raceway and Watkins Glen as well. All in all I danced with her on 35 tracks and she was quick and reliable on almost every outing.

Along the way she and I were written up in several vintage magazines. No less than Burt Levy, after sharing an enduro drive at Road America in the fall of 2003, called her *"a lovely and user-friendly little machine with a delightful personality"* and from that event Classic Motorsports magazine selected us "Pick of the Liter".

For the first few years she was my only Lotus. As I got to know her, a fully captivating process. I came to admire the amazing thought process that created this little car. Classed as C production (A being the top class) even though it had a motor that was smaller than the E production MGB and Triumph, she ran lap times equal with Porsche 911's, AP Corvettes and BP Mustangs. How on earth was this even possible? I read the history of Lotus; of Colin Chapman and his merry band of overachievers. I was blown away at what this tiny team accomplished in producing not only class busting road cars but in creating winning sports racers and F1 champions. As I learned more, I created a wish-list of other Lotus cars I wanted to own and experience.

First came the Elite – such a pretty car but also a technological marvel. After looking at more than a dozen, I found an unrestored original up in Washington in 1999. She is called the Princess and has been with me and Ann on two big rallies; the Texas 1000 and the Copperstate. What a lovely little car! Shortly thereafter I acquired the S3 Seven that has been my faithful companion on at least six trips of over 1,000 miles each, then an M100 Elan, a Europa Special and an Esprit Turbo. I couldn't afford my dream sports racer, the Lotus 23, but was able to acquire a Westfield version of an Eleven, and then followed an early Elan Coupe'. Finally, I found an Elan Plus 2, my sweet little Elan S2, a 5/8th scale Seven, and another S3 Elan basket case that I sold on to a friend who is bringing it back to life. And to round out the collection, I caved and bought a four seater Lotus; an Eclat with a Rover V8 engine transplant

Ultimately I have owned 12 different Lotus cars and still have 4 and 5/8 in the garage. I'm not done yet either…an Evora is calling me. But the first and most memorable was my Elan racecar. They say Lotus cars are fragile – yet all this happened because a Sprite kept breaking axles.

3 YOU PICKED A FINE TIME...

This is a story about a couple of guys, a car and a song. If the car weren't old and British, it would have made a great country song.

It all started in August 1984, when my friend Wiley Smith and I made plans to go to the first ever Rocky Mountain Vintage Race in Steamboat Springs, Colorado over Labor Day weekend. We were pretty excited about seeing racing 300SL's and Cobras.... well you get the idea. I only had a mere Austin Healey 3000, and hoped I wouldn't feel humbled with all the high priced exotics we expected to see. Even in the four months I'd had my car, I'd learned enough to worry about Healey overheating, especially handling 12,000 foot high Berthoud Pass. I suggested we take his E type Jaguar, but, believe it or not, we took the Healey for the larger luggage space. Labor Day weekend came with a heat wave, but Wiley promised, from his half vast previous Healey experience, that overheating wouldn't be a problem.

So, in 95 degree heat, we left work early to beat the traffic. We didn't. Stuck in the slow grind of the rush hour (Why do they call it that? Obviously no one rushes), I watched the temperature gauge rise ever upward to 212 and climbing as fast as we were on the first long grade out of town. I thought we'd better stop, but Wiley's logic was that we were starting to move faster on the less crowded highway and headed for cool mountain air. As long as we had power we probably weren't doing any harm. We kept going. The temp rose. 212. 215. 220. We kept going. Finally, the temp gauge started to drift downward, oh so slowly, and at last held steady about 195. The relief I felt on a beautiful day, a great road and a good running British car was: Ecstasy? Euphoria? At least, contentment? Needless to say, the trip up and over the top of the pass was a kick on a beautiful day in a beautiful car.

After we had handled a dozen hairpin turns on the way up the pass, we still had a like quota to conquer coming down. After the first couple of long, gentle sweeping arcs, we approached the first really hard turn, a left hander which required substantial slowing. I stepped on the brakes and heard the most bizarre sound, and felt the weirdest vibration. The noise was a blend of scraping fingernails on a blackboard and chains rattling. I let off the brake, almost simultaneously downshifted, and said to a perplexed Wiley; "What the Hell was that?" The noise and vibration had stopped, so I knew he was guessing when he said nervously, "Waterpump?" Nonetheless it sounded logical after the heat we'd been through. We were fast approaching a sharp right curve as well as the car ahead of us so I hit the brakes again, hard this time, and got the same sound, same vibration. Before I said a word, I heard a thunk, felt a thump and began bouncing along on the right front suspension parts.

They say, before you die, the whole of your life flashes before your eyes. All I saw was my right front wheel flashing before my eyes. It rolled straight in front of the car for about a hundred feet, curved gently across the highway, up the embankment on the left side, back down the embankment, back across the highway, disappearing down the steep hill to the right. It didn't hit a thing! Meanwhile, I was bringing the car to rest on what the Colorado Highway Dept. cheerfully describes as a shoulder. Other than needing a change of underwear, we were unhurt. But what about my precious Healey?

As I began to survey the damage, and try to figure out what went wrong, Wiley went looking for the wheel and other miscellaneous parts. Apparently, the splines on the right front wheel were so worn that when I braked heavily, the hub stopped turning but the wheel continued to rotate. The result was that the friction of the wheel against the knockoff, had literally unscrewed the knockoff. (So that's what UNDO means!)

It looked like bad news/good news. The bad news was obvious: the fender was dented and bore the famous Healey fender spear except in the wrong place, traced in black rubber. The brake disc was flattened on the bottom, sort of horseshoe shaped where it had ridden locked in combat with the pavement. And finally, I saw grit and sand packed into every crevice of the suspension. The good news took a bit more reflection; we were OK, Wiley had found the wheel and knock off, and I had a fairly complete tool kit.

We decided to see if we could get things enough together to make it to a mechanic or garage. To pass the time we began humming and singing, to keep from cursing. Soon I had a tune pop into my head, and somehow began "the song".

To the tune of the Kenny Rogers song "Lucille" I began singing:

> *"You picked a fine time to leave me, loose wheel.*
> *Just when we thought things were no great big deal.*
> *We'll probably miss Steamboat,*
> *Stuck here with this dreamboat,*
> *Unless we can get things to heal.*
> *You picked a fine time to leave me loose wheel".*

Over and over, as we cleaned, reassembled, filed, banged, tightened and twisted all the parts into their approximate original positions, we sang that demented song. We were done, we'd relaxed and the car had cooled down. It was time to give it a try.

Gingerly, I let off the brake, put the shift lever into first, let the clutch out, and prayed. It all worked! Then I stepped on the brake again and heard a familiar sound. This time I knew exactly what it was so I grabbed the emergency brake and brought us to a ragged stop. Now what? Either toward Steamboat or back home to Denver we faced a seven thousand foot descent in a car that worked fine as long as I didn't use the brakes! Swell!

So I did what any rookie Healey owner would do…I drove the fifty miles back to Denver without using the foot brake. I slowed as much as possible with the gears and then used the handbrake since it didn't affect the front wheels.

Well we made it safely back home, selected about half the gear to transfer to the Jag and headed back to Steamboat. Through the cool night with the full moon and light traffic, we really put the hammer down and we definitely made up some lost time (Healey speed plus about 30 - 40 knots) saw some wonderful cars and racing, and scarcely thought of the project waiting for my return. The whole right front suspension was shot. And so were all the rest of the splines. I had to replace it all, but that's an entirely different story. So let's take this one from the top again. All together now, "You picked a fine time........"

4 GOOD NEWS AND BAD NEWS

Stupid and naïve are not the same, although the results may be. While the plan my friend Jim Hegy and I made to take our cars to the Chicago Historic races wasn't quite the "Hold my beer and watch this!" variety of stupid, it wasn't much more fully formed, so the best that could be said was that we were naïve to expect a smooth trip. Perhaps I should start at the beginning.

Jim and I had been friends for about ten years. I met him in a gas station with the hood up on his Austin Healey. This was not an isolated incident; in fact it was a very common sight for all his friends to see with Jim. There are dozens of stories I could tell you, if you will provide the beer, that illustrate how Jim digs a metaphorical hole during some outing with a car and then by some great, good fortune gets out of the mess with only a small inconvenience. Like the time Jim was the only one of a dozen or so who didn't refuel at a gas stop just before Glenwood Canyon then ran out 30 miles later right in the canyon where there are NO services, then got a tow to a gas station in Glenwood Springs. The point of this background is to set the stage for a complex trip that we naïvely assumed would go well.

We had been vintage racing together for about four years, both starting in the Spridget class and both graduating to faster more capable cars since. Jim had a Turner 1500 and I had a Lotus Elan. We had been to all the tracks within Colorado, and a few further afield, and thinking that we had mastered these and in 1996, looking for bigger challenges, decided on a road trip. But where?

There are lots of road course tracks around the country that are fun to drive and then there are the icons of the sport where so much history has been written and our heroes have driven. Among these are Watkins Glen, Sebring and Road Atlanta in the east, Laguna Seca, Sears Point and Pacific Raceways in the west, and Mid-Ohio and Road America in the Midwest. Based on our schedule and the events scheduled, we settled on the Chicago Historic races at Road America.

Ahh, Elkhart Lake Wisconsin. Famous course, great beer, sublime brats and fantastic cars. It was a worthy goal so we set about the required logistics to make it happen. First, the entry forms were duly filled out and sent in and, happily, both were accepted. Then came plans for getting the two of us plus friend Dennis Hall and our two cars the 1,200 miles to Elkhart and back.

Jim has a 28 foot enclosed trailer that comfortably holds the Elan and Turner, and an old Chevy Suburban to pull it. Now this Suburban, while it has the "Big Block" engine, also has 190,000 miles on it as we depart Denver so Jim wants to take it easy. Our concern with this plan was the old, tired truck … there are 1,200 miles between Denver and Elkhart Lake Wisconsin. Thus our perfectly conceived plan was to leave after work on Thursday night and arrive Friday mid-day ready to sign in and get some practice. We loaded the trailer on Tuesday evening and packed our personal gear so Thursday at about 5:30 we were on our way. The first few hours were uneventful. We cruised along the Interstate into Nebraska at a comfortable 65 or so and even stopped for a break. In fact, it was so calm rolling along the comment from Jim didn't even register at first. He said "That's funny, the radio quit" followed shortly by "I think the lights are dimming". We pulled over to the shoulder and checked underhood. The alternator was shot.

We were in the middle of Nebraska, the sun was almost fully set, and the nearest town was about 30 miles east. What to do? With no alternator we had to run on the battery so, using only parking lights to identify that we were actually there, we began following a semi-trailer truck at 70 mph. Since we couldn't see where we were going with our own non-functional headlights, Jim, the metaphorical hole digger, figured it would be safe to tow a 7,000 pound trailer in the dark fifty feet behind a semi at that speed. Somehow, we made it safely to Kearney, Nebraska.

We left our escort and peeled down an exit ramp to a truck stop which serviced the big rigs, hoping they could help us with a new alternator.

With almost no battery life left, Jim managed to park in the lot near the service bay and we got out to assess the situation. The first problem was that the repair place worked on big rigs and as big as our rig was to us, it wasn't even a little rig to them, so they carried no parts. The second problem was that most of the parts stores in the big time city of Kearney, Nebraska closed at 9:00 and it was now 9:30.

Luckily, Jim has an angel that sends out "help me" vibes in situations like these. The guy at the truck stop was personal friends with the owner of the NAPA store in town, knew where he would be after closing and called him at the 19th Hole Bar and Grill. The owner finished his beer went back to the NAPA store, got the proper alternator, and delivered it to the truck stop. Meanwhile, the help, Bubba as we named him, proceeded to try to remove the broken alternator and put the Suburban battery on a charger. We named him because he was the embodiment of all the clichés about the big, slow, farm boy with the sweat stained seed cap and overalls. You know the kind that, with a bit bigger IQ, become down linemen for Nebraska football and win national championships.

Jim had tried to remove the alternator but the bolt was stuck and while he went to find some penetrating oil, Bubba thought he'd give it a try. Jim was just returning to the scene when he spied Bubba and, worried that Bubba might use a bit too much force, yelled "Be careful of the mounting...it could break", which it did right about at the word "could". Jim calmly surveyed the pieces and determined that the alternator could be held on with a smaller bolt than the ½" original, ultimately using a 10-32 machine screw which remained in there until 2009 I think. The replaced alternator seemed to work fine, so at about 11:00PM we headed to Wisconsin.

Rolling along through the night we took turns sleeping in the back seat or the reclined passenger seat of the Suburban, trading off at intervals of about 2 hours per driving stint. Unbelievably, the Suburban ran fine all through the night through Iowa and Wisconsin. When we reached Road America we were both exhausted and impressed. What a place! Compared to our little club tracks, the place is like Madison Square Garden versus the local Elks Club. It's like being at a two thousand acre national park with home cooking and a race track in the middle. The church group food stands provide the best track food in the country – hotcakes, brats, potato salad, corn on the cob and more are all made with loving care the way your mom would if she were there. And the track lap is four miles and flows like an asphalt stream over the terrain. We were properly intimidated, and being tired made it even more intimidating.

Not only is Road America one of the longest tracks in the country, it is one of the oldest. While other classic tracks have gone (Bridgehampton, Marlboro, and Meadowdale) and others have been significantly altered, (Laguna Seca, Sebring) this wonderful manifestation of Cliff Tufte's dedication is still here in all its glory as it originated. And the way the course drapes over the Kettle Moraine hills make it one of the most fun tracks there is to drive. From the high speed sweep of turn one where we can carry way more speed than we think, to the hard braking into turn five, the rhythm of Hurry Downs, the oil pressure and neck straining length of the Carousel and the balancing act that is the Kink – all this and the climb up the hill from Canada corner make this track hugely memorable to anyone who is lucky enough to get to drive here. With history that goes back to the mid-fifties, every one of our heroes raced here on what is essentially the same track. Now we would get to play on this historic asphalt.

When we unloaded among a group of other small bore racers we found a friendly group who helped us find our way to tech inspection, the fuel pumps and the pre-grid. It is tough getting into the flow of a race weekend at a strange track especially after an all-nighter so having kindly fellow racers who knew the ropes was a real blessing. Still, we started slowly because of our lack of track knowledge. Jim was in a different race group than I was so I was first on track. What a rush to carry speed for as long and fast as I ever had – it was nothing like our home tracks. But getting to good lap times means committing the car at what are very high speed corners like turn 1, the Carousel and the Kink, and that takes repetition plus a lot of courage. Thus we each started at the back of our respective groups.

What was a fun run for me was a disaster for Jim. First his fiberglass bonnet/hood came undone at the front, caught the wind and broke off the hinges, flying over his head and off the track. Black flagged, he came in after only a couple of laps giving a whole new meaning to "hood up". The next session, with a thoroughly duct taped bonnet, his water pump failed and he overheated after one lap. Calling on his angel once again, he found a fellow in the paddock selling a Formula Ford engine, talked the guy into loaning him the water pump and it's Gilmer drive belt and pulleys, exchanged it all in the grass where we were parked with the hood up. Two sessions and only three laps meant starting from the back yet again. Finally he got in a full session. Meanwhile I was learning the course and where I could really push the car. Though our practice was done, my times kept improving so I had high hopes for qualifying for Sunday's race. The key to getting faster is track time, and we had little.

When it was time to qualify, the rain came. Now, in Colorado we rarely see rain and *never* race in rain, so, on an unfamiliar track with unfamiliar drivers and how they behave, I thought it best to sit out the session. Without a qualifying time, I started 54th out of 62 cars. I was about eighth fastest based on practice times but I started behind all those with any qualifying time at all. By the time Jim's qualifying session came, the rain had passed and the track had dried. He qualified 22nd out of about 60 cars – quite respectable for as little as he had been on track.

We went out to Siebkens Resort with Dennis, who had helped us both in getting the cars to the grid and with Jim's water pump replacement, for a nice dinner and to relax. The highlight for all of us was the visit to the Siebkens bar. The bar is small and not very fancy but was crowded with racers as it has been for fifty years whenever a race weekend comes round. There was a palpable energy in the place where the spirits of past drivers mixed with the spirits served that night for a heady mixture of awestruck camaraderie. It was almost as if we could sense the presence of Andretti, Foyt, Gurney, Hall, and dozens of other famous names from the past.

Sunday dawned bright and clear. Both cars ran well during the morning warm-up so we were pumped up for our afternoon races. I went out first, and quickly moved through the backmarkers to about the 20th spot. Then it got harder but more satisfying to pick off cars under braking into turn 5 or Canada Corner or get a jump out of turn 14 to enable a pass before the hill. The car was more and more comfortable and I found more and more speed as the race progressed. All too soon the checkered flag fell, just as I was hitting my stride, feeling at one with the car and track. At the end of the race I was 8th and felt a nice glow of achievement. Then it was Jim's turn.

For once, Jim finished the entire session about where he qualified and without problems. He came in with a big grin on his face for the first time this weekend. We were set to roll his car right into the trailer where mine was already tied down and hit the road back to Denver until Jim reminded us that he had to return the water pump to the fellow who had loaned it to him. And before the pump could be removed the water temp had to cool down - for about 45 minutes. Once it was cooled it took another hour to remove the parts, replace the old ones and load the car.

We left an almost deserted paddock as the place had emptied while we burned daylight waiting to become cool…actually, almost a metaphor for our trip but we didn't yet know that. We finally left about 6:30 pm.

Our return plan was, like the repair manuals say, the reverse of the outbound trip...drive through the night and be back in Denver by Monday evening ready to go to work on Tuesday morning. As we rolled through Wisconsin into Iowa, we took turns napping and at the wheel. Fast food just as it was getting dark kept us fueled through the night. Somewhere in the dark of an Iowa midnight as I was dozing in the right seat and Dennis was asleep in the back, Jim quietly said "Oh Sh!t!" It was so softly stated it was terrifying. I bolted straight upright and asked what was wrong. "Well", he said, "I'm pressing down on the accelerator pedal and the revs are rising but we are slowing down". That couldn't be good of course so Jim pulled off to the side of the Interstate onto the shoulder and put the gear selector into "Park". The whole rig started to coast backwards. Slamming on the brakes Jim said one clear word – "Transmission!"

Someplace in the middle of Iowa and the middle of the night, our trip had come to a sudden halt. Dennis asked Jim where we were and Jim ventured "Iowa?" Realizing that we needed real help, I handed my cell phone to Jim and told him to dial 911. Though I could only hear Jim's end of the conversation it was easy to tell that the operator needed something more specific in terms of our location in order to send help. So, wearing a navy blue sweatshirt and jeans no less, Dennis set off in the pitch black night along the shoulder of the interstate to find a mile marker while I took my camera with long lens and climbed the steep bank to see if I could use it like a telescope and read a road sign. I saw a sign back to the east for a restaurant and a flashing beacon at an airport along with an exit whose name and number I couldn't quite make out. Returning to the car, I passed this info on to Jim who called the 911 operator again. With these clues, she said she knew right where we were...between the two Newton Iowa exits. She said a state trooper was handling another incident west of us and that he would be there as soon as he finished that. We waited.

After what seemed like hours but was probably only 20 minutes, Dennis suddenly emerged out of the full darkness and said "I found mile marker 165 and based on how long it took to get back here I estimate we are at mile 165 and a 1/2". We accepted his estimate and told him he was very close. We were, in fact, at mile marker 165.51 which was on a post about one foot in front of the right headlight of the Suburban. It seems that Iowa marks every reflector post with a location mileage, a piece of information we learned from the 911 operator but only on the second call well after Dennis had left! We waited some more.

Sometime later the trooper pulled up and sternly said immediately, "Show me what's in the trailer!" which we willingly did. It seems there had been a rash of incidents where illegal aliens were being transported in old trailers pulled by old cars and we fit the profile. After satisfying himself that we really were "car guys" with a problem, he became very friendly and helpful. He called for a tow and after another long wait a big wrecker came, hooked up the Suburban with trailer still attached and took us into Newton to his storage yard where we were to wait until the local Chevy dealership opened in the morning. We tried to sleep but with the windows up it was too hot and with them down, swatting the mosquitos kept us awake. We waited some more.

We had disconnected the trailer at about 7:00 am so the tow truck hooked up the detached Suburban and delivered it and us to the dealer shop. We waited some more. Finally, the Chevy folks came to work. With the shop pickup they pushed the Suburban over to the lift then Jim went to the customer lounge to find us. So Jim, Dennis and I conferred. We all had to get back to Denver to our work and families but it was quite clear we weren't going in the Suburban that day. We hadn't eaten anything since leaving Wisconsin so I asked to borrow the dealership truck and make a breakfast run to some fast food place in town then we'd talk about options over breakfast. The first place I found was a Hardee's which has even more yummy cholesterol in every bite than McDonald's. While I waited for the food, an idea occurred to me. Back with the guys, as we wolfed down the melted grease, I made my suggestion. Since we had started out from Elkhart Lake the night before and driven straight though to Newton, it was quite possible that we were ahead of several other Coloradoans who had also been at Road America if they had stopped for the night. So I suggested I take the truck out to the first Newton exit and see if anyone came by in the next hour while Jim negotiated the terms of the replacement transmission and Dennis made calls. Everyone agreed. I guess none of us really believed I would find a ride or the next obvious questions would have been raised. Then what? Who goes and who stays?

I parked the loaner truck at the terminus of the off ramp and walked down to the ramp entrance where I stared into oncoming westbound traffic trying to spot a familiar vehicle with Colorado plates. For about twenty minutes I saw nothing hopeful but then a racer from Omaha that I knew had been at the event came by, honked and waved. So there was hope, since one person at least had stopped for the night and was behind us. Another 15 minutes passed. I thought chances had faded but then I saw a familiar camper with a trailer; it was Brian and Anita Nightengale. I began jumping up and down and waving my arms frantically hoping to be seen. As they came closer I watched Anita do a classic double take…first seeing some nut doing jumping jacks by the freeway and then realizing she knew that nut!

As Brian slowed to a stop on the shoulder, I ran to the door of the motorhome. After explaining what had happened, asking for a ride back to Denver and hearing a yes, I now had to get back to the dealership, gather my gear and whoever else was coming and get back to the Interstate exit. Brian said that he hadn't yet showered and would do that until I came back. I ran up the ramp and drove back to the dealership.

Even more resolved to not spend another day in Newton, I made a statement to Jim he has never let me live down. I said, "I have good news and bad news, which do you want first?" He said "Give me the good news." I replied, "Here's $70 which is all the money I have and it is yours. The bad news is I have a ride back to Denver and you are on your own!" Dennis said, "I have more bad news Jim, I'm going with him!" Jim just shook his head and grimaced.

Gentleman that he is, Jim drove us to the waiting motorhome and wished us well. The drive back to Denver was uneventful in the Nightengale's well-maintained rig and the kindness of our fellow racers was again demonstrated by them. Both Dennis and I were home by sundown and, as we had originally planned, could be at work on Tuesday morning.

Meanwhile, back in Newton, at the shop, I learned that in our absence Jim had been waiting most of the day for the one mechanic who had special training in transmissions to finish another car. First, the mechanic who was trained on transmission stuff had an appointment for a root canal for which he just up and left, leaving the job barely started. When Jim checked with the service manager about why no one was working on the car, he was told that Mr. Toothache was the only one qualified to do the work and he was gone for the appointment. An entire morning and half the afternoon were lost. When he heard this Jim bugged the owner to have someone look at it so the owner told another mechanic took a look. After half an hour, he came to the waiting room with the specific technical diagnosis: "It's your transmission. It's broke!" Well with a solid diagnosis like that one, which was much more specific and detailed that our crude amateur guess, eight hours earlier Jim was left with one question – "Can you fix it?" The answer was no. A rebuilt unit would need to come from Chicago and that would mean tomorrow at least.

The next morning the owner reported that it would be two days to get the transmission there and one to install it so the earliest Jim could go to Denver would be Friday night. Three days in Newton! Jim stayed in a cheap motel and watched "I Love Lucy" reruns waiting for the transmission. When it finally came it wasn't just bolt in in and go either - Oh, no.

When the transmission was completely installed, the Suburban lowered on the lift and started up, there was no movement of the vehicle no matter what gear was selected. The only "qualified" mechanic suggested it must be a bad rebuilt unit and told Jim they would have to order another one. Having spent quite enough time in scenic downtown Newton, Jim, who is a pretty knowledgeable mechanic in his own right, said no to ordering another transmission without a thorough check of this one. So they put it back up on the lift, and dropped the pan. When they had done so, it was clear that there was no fluid pickup tube on the rebuilt unit. The rebuilder's intent was clearly to use the pickup tube from the old unit as it was not something that breaks. Why the expert didn't know this no one could say. It was Newton Iowa though so maybe Bubba isn't just a Nebraska boy. Once the pickup tube was in place, the transmission worked just fine so Jim paid up, took off to hook up the trailer and head for Colorado.

After driving a few blocks, Jim got to thinking that while he was watching, nobody had refilled the transmission fluid after putting the pan back on. While there was enough fluid to run the torque converter, there certainly wasn't enough to cool and replenish operation for 900 miles of towing in the summer heat. Stopping at the next exit he added almost two quarts of transmission fluid, saving another total disaster. Once again the amateur mechanic trumped the professional so called "expert". After the top up of fluid the Suburban ran perfectly and Jim was home about sundown on Friday after a lonely week in Newton and a long, tiring, solo drive. Fortunately, he was well rested from his Iowa vacation.

We have laughed about that trip many, many times over the years and added many more "Jim Stories" to the ledger of adventures with cars, but the phrase that still makes Jim wince is this: "I've got good news and bad news..."

5 LITTLE CAR – BIG TRIP

I was racing my vintage Elan S2 at the Northwest Historics in Seattle in July 2000, and saw "the car" a 1968 Lotus Seven S3, at the Lotus Corral in the paddock between races.

While I had wanted a Seven for a while, the price was a little higher than I had budgeted, and I was uncertain about whether I wanted a right hand drive car. I wasn't quite ready to act. About two weeks later I got a phone call from a friend in the Evergreen Lotus Club saying that Bob, the owner, was going to sell the car at a very attractive price to a guy who had had low balled him because it was the only offer he had. The number was *well* below the previous price. He said, "If you'll make Bob a little better offer he'll sell to you and the car will go to a good home". I did...and, as they say, the rest is history.

However, I still had to collect the car and get it home to Denver. So, I tried to get it shipped and even thought about taking my race trailer up to Snohomish, a pretty little town just north of Seattle and retrieving it, but finally decided I needed a little adventure. Since God protects drunks and fools, after several beers I made a one-way reservation and flew up to Seattle on September 2nd, 2000. My daughter, Rebecca who lives there, met me at the airport and drove me to Snohomish and the waiting seller. After an hour spent with Bob familiarizing me with the things he knew and after giving Rebecca a short ride, I stopped in "downtown" Snohomish (Pop 8,400) at a Quick Lube for oil and filter, fluid check, and to hit the lube points. At about 4:00 I started off on highway 2 towards Wenatchee, my destination in Denver only 1,350 miles away in a tiny, topless, right hand drive car about which I really knew nothing.

I drove upward through evergreen hills on a great winding road next to a stream, and over Stevens pass, through a light shower, then continued on to Moses Lake where I stopped for the night. A very pleasant and smooth, but also pretty short, first day. So far, so good!

In the morning, I zigzagged across eastern Washington, specifically through the town of Kahlotus, requiring a stop at the "general store" for a soft drink in celebration of the name, and then over the Snake River gorge and into Lewiston, Idaho. There I picked up US 12 across the hump of Idaho, on 200 of the most beautiful miles of road I've ever driven. US 12 follows the river up to the top of a pass and another river down the other side, weaving and bobbing like the river adjacent, but with smooth asphalt instead of water. There are roads that make us grin because they suit the car we have, and this road, Highway 12 in Idaho, like Highway 2 in Washington is a definite 'Grin Road" And with almost no traffic to break the rhythm of the curves, I was just grinning the whole way. As to why there was no traffic that would become very clear a bit later.

At Lolo Montana, I stopped for gas and noticed oil coating the rear of the car. Checking underneath, I found an axle seal leaking, and with no seal in my spares, I did what any owner of an old British car would do... just topped up the diff, and kept going. By the time I reached Denver I'd used more than 2 quarts of 90 wt. The gas stop in Lolo marked the end of the eastern traverse over passes and through flat farmland. Now, I would turn south and run through the valleys of Idaho with long ranges of snow capped mountains on both sides.

As I drove south through the Bitterroot Valley, two things awed me. The valley is one of the most spectacular places I've ever seen and parts were burned beyond belief. In the summer of 2000 fires were rampant throughout the west as it was one of the hottest summers on record in the Northwest. As one of the largest, the fire in the Bitterroot Valley meant that Hot Shots, the gypsy bands of what we used to call "smoke jumpers", had come from all over the country to attack this big fire. Hundreds of firefighters were visible just a 1/4-mile off the road. The light green Forest Service pumper fire trucks and equipment were the only vehicles coming north for over 90 minutes with no one going south. I was told that they had just opened the highway south two hours earlier. The acrid smell of burning and the blackened forest were testament to the power of nature. These Hot Shots might be used to this but I was no hotshot so I felt puny and alone.

Onward I went to my evening destination, Salmon, Idaho, the largest town between Montana and Rexburg, ID near Wyoming, but still a town of only about 6,000 people. When I arrived about nightfall, I found that there were no rooms left within 60 miles. All were taken by firefighters. A fire Captain in the gas station said there were rooms in Challis, Idaho about 63 miles away. He was certain of this because he had just sent two of his men there. My target became Challis. As I got ready to leave, he warned me to be sure not to take the left fork onto Idaho 28 because there was nothing for 122 miles that way. So I filled my gas tank, my differential, and my stomach, and headed south.

Off I blasted, air temperature dropping into the 40's and the clear sky clouding over from the Southwest. As I drove, it got darker and colder, even with the heat coming off the engine filling the foot well. The stars were magnificent since there was no, and I mean NO, ambient light. Well, that made the line of clouds even more distinct driving south. After about 45 minutes, and having seen no other cars going either way, I was concerned about where I was in relation to Challis. I finally saw a route marker...Idaho 28. I had taken the wrong fork! Hoo Boy! There would be nothing for another 80 miles ahead, or I could go back 40 miles and then south 60 more. Nothing to do but proceed. About then I felt so much more tiny and insignificant, I was glad that God protects fools, too.

Another car's headlights became visible in my mirror and that was reassuring. After a long time he finally caught up to me and passed. I was happy to have a car to follow through the dark night but he cut back into the right lane so sharply that his "strafing" move startled me and I lifted off the gas pedal abruptly. When I resumed my previous throttle setting, the car ran roughly and seemed to have lost power. The revs began falling slowly as the taillights of the car that had passed, the only car I'd seen in 45 minutes, disappeared over a low rise.

My car was barely able to sustain speed and I was certain that something major had failed leaving me to fend for myself in wild, rural Idaho. I could picture the headline: *"Idiot found frozen in Lotus position, half eaten by Bear"*. As I struggled to maintain forward motion and came over the rise I saw a mercury vapor light ahead. A farm or ranch with kindhearted people, I hoped. It was, in fact, a crossroads with a tavern, a closed general store and several dark buildings. As I coasted to a stop and untangled myself from the Seven, I was startled by the presence of people behind me. I had been wearing earplugs, (not a complete fool) so the four teenagers were quite close before I heard them.. Again, my mind fashioned a headline *"Rural gang dismembers old man foolish enough to be driving an ancient Lotus with Lucas electrics - well after dark"*

It turns out they were great kids who had heard the car struggling and saw it stop under the light, and now wanted to see it up close. I explained my predicament, and wondered aloud if there were a warm place to catch some sleep and work on the car in the morning. One eager lad suggested I check at the Motel in "town". Where, asked I? Right there, said he, as he pointed to a dark house just across the intersection. So I went up and dutifully knocked on the door.

A light came on inside, illuminating a man who had clearly fallen asleep in front of the TV, who then staggered to the door turning on the porch light. This, in turn, illuminated the "No Vacancy" sign. I remarked on the sign and was about to request the porch floor when he said, "Oh, Mother always forgets that. I think we have one left." Thinking he may be related to Norman Bates, I was relieved when "Mother" turned out to be his wife who ran the business. She sent me to a tiny cabin out behind the house usually rented to hunters and fishermen. In the Seven I sputtered around the main house to an ice cold cabin. It had a propane wall heater that finally scorched the temperature up to almost 60 degrees. I'd deal with car problems in the morning. I was exhausted.

Morning dawned clear and bright with a new blanket of snow on the mountains ringing this long valley. There was no fire evident here and the fall colors were beautiful. If only I didn't still have over 700 miles to go and a crippled car. There was frost on the car, but the sun was warming things so I took off the bonnet to have a look. The first thing that jumped out at me was a hose from the block up to the intake manifold that had popped out of a hole in the block. Well, it could be this I thought, as I looked around for other possible problems. I put the hose back in and noted that the other end went into the manifold below the carburetor. It was the PCV hose, and I realized the intake manifold would have been sucking air in after the fuel was mixed in the carb, resulting in a very lean mixture. No wonder it wouldn't run right! As I fired it up it ran great. I felt smug and breathed a sigh of relief. Man solved! It ran beautifully the rest of the trip.

Down through Idaho, into Wyoming, the scenery was spectacular -the snowcapped peaks, evergreen forests and rolling foothills up and through Driggs, Idaho. The two lane roads were lightly traveled and the weather was a perfect 65 degrees and sunny. Over the pass, through the Grand

Tetons, the Seven was in its element; with a rhythm and flow that one writer calls "Road Dancing". Another "Grin Road"! The winding curves led me right into Jackson Hole. There I stopped for a very pleasant lunch of a great cheeseburger and a beer. Sitting on the deck in the sun, looking over the railing at the little Seven that got me here I felt one of those rare moments of real bliss.

As I sipped my beer and contemplated the Seven I realized it wasn't much of a car; some tubes and sheet aluminum, an engine, four wheels with fiberglass wings, and two seats, yet it was all anyone really needed. It got me here in good style and with luck would get me home to Denver.

I forced myself to get out of my comfortable reverie and get going again down Highway 191 south to the town of Pinedale. For some 75 miles it was lovely, but then it became rocky buttes and brown, dry, scrub brush. I was spit out of the beauty onto the ugly high prairie toward (yuck) Rock Springs. For the next 230 miles the Wyoming wind tried to rip my head right off my neck. This was the worst part of the trip; one for which the Seven is ill suited. The Grin Roads were gone, replaced by Grim Roads for 230 miles. I needed a hardtop and a fifth gear. I had neither.

To get from Rock Springs to a southerly road into Colorado, requires 175 miles on Interstate 80 with the big trucks. Really Big, Fast, Trucks! I stayed in the right lane at about 65-mph, and hugged the right line as semis went by, trying to suck me into their wake. Looking up at the wheel centers of the big trailers impressed upon me again that I would be but a speed bump if they ran over me. As hard as I was pushing it seemed ironic that I could have driven under most of the trailers and hooked on for a free ride! Just before I was to finally turn off the big slab onto southbound two lane highway 130, a Wyoming Trooper stopped me. He hadn't seen a license plate from the westbound lane in his mirror, so he turned around and gave chase. After checking turn signals and brake lights, he admitted that he just wanted to see "what in the hell that little car was, anyway". We talked awhile and he wished me well and told me "to be careful next to those big trucks!" As if I needed to be reminded.

The rest of the trip was delightful. Highway 130 became a Grin Road called Highway 230 south of Saratoga and stayed that way as I crossed into Colorado. On what was now Colorado 125, the grins continued until I stopped for a late lunch in Walden. Thoreau's Walden was a bit different, yet the serenity and beauty must have been similar. He wanted to let go of a complicated life and get back to simpler things. I'm sure in the year 2000 the Seven would have filled that premise.

Through Granby and Winter Park on US 40 I grinned and at Berthoud Pass went over the Continental Divide at 11,500 feet and ran solid and true right on into Denver…grinning all the way.

I was home safe and sound after three and a half days and five states. And, most amazingly of all, I had travelled 1,350 miles in an old, small, unfamiliar, right hand drive car with no top or weather protection, and without major problems, through some of the most remote space in this country. Remote space that was on fire no less! Everywhere I stopped people were both cheerful and friendly; charmed by this simple, little, open car. They asked at every stop where I had come from and where I was going. When I told them there was usually a low whistle and a head shake as they expressed encouragement for the journey and delight with the car. At the same time their delight was mixed with doubt about my sanity. I almost got a sense of their wistfulness that they didn't have the chutzpah to give it a go. I wasn't sure at first either, but, in retrospect, it was the most memorable trip I had ever taken. Until I took the next one, but that's another story!

The Seven, at rest in our driveway, looks ready to take another Road Trip!

6 THE TEXAS 1000 ELITE

A friend of mine asked me, "What kind of idiot would drive a thousand miles, to drive a thousand miles, to drive a thousand miles home?"

The answer, apparently, is one like me. Exactly like me, in fact. And what is more, it may be one of the most fun things I've done with any of our Lotuses outside of vintage racing.

I have driven our 1960 Lotus Elite regularly since I acquired it in the fall of 1999 and by the fall of 2002 I decided to have it refreshed to get it more roadworthy. The engine was tired and so was the gearbox and since I had acquired a ZF transmission with the car, albeit in a separate crate, and I had acquired a pair of SU carbs on a manifold from Elite expert Dennis Ortenburger, and a four branch exhaust manifold from Hutton Engineering in Clarksville, TN, I decided it was time to put all the pieces together in what was to be essentially an SE specification Elite.

So over the next 10 months, I had the top end of the engine freshened, (the bottom end was thought to be fine) with a steel cam gear added, the engine compartment repainted and the ZF and SU's added. I figured that I would now be road ready. Well as soon as we get cocky, the world has a way of reminding us that we only think we are in control of our destiny. A delivery truck blindly backed into the left rear of the Elite. At least the fellow accepted responsibility, saying "I never saw it; it's so...little!" So, as long as we had to do the repair and paint that area, I bit the bullet and added the rest of the car to the paint order. So the long and short was that the car was road ready only the weekend before we were ready to tow to Texas. No problem...it's a Road Trip!

On October 27, 2003 my girlfriend Ann and I took the Elite and my race Elan and headed for Texas World Speedway. Our plan was to race the weekend event there with the race prepared Elan, using the Elite as our local transportation to and from the motel, and then to begin the Texas 1000 rally with it on Monday the 3rd of November. We found the Elite to be great both in town and on the freeway out to the track. We were able to get up into the 80-90 mph range on several occasions. The car was somehow sweeter and had more power than I remembered, and the ZF transmission made a huge difference in the character of the car with its rifle bolt like action. I loved the Elite even more than before.

The cars in the rally got to "tour" the TWS road course as a group and, because I knew the track from the race meet, I was able to hound a 427 Corvette for two laps. The Elite felt good: stable and forgiving with a bit of understeer. It gave us confidence for the rally and in the next four days of driving we added another 1,065 miles.

The Texas 1000 is really more a "tour" than a true rally. While there were checkpoints, they were only at the end of a stage, and the time to reach them was usually ample if one could follow directions, not necessarily a justified assumption. The spirit of the thing is more a group of friends zipping around the scenic back roads with a wonderful hotel and food waiting at the end of each day, than it is a "real" rally. Even the lunch stops were at fabulous places.

We started from the Driskill Hotel in Austin, TX. Built in 1886 to be the "best hotel in America" by cattle baron Jesse Driskill and beautifully restored, it is one of the prestigious Historic Hotels of America on the National Trust for Historic Preservation.

We had a whole floor of their parking garage reserved for the tour cars. That's where we first met the owners of the various cars going on the tour as we prepared and polished our entrant. We found a Porsche 911RS, a Peerless Coupe, a Morgan Plus 8, Aston Martin DB5 Drophead, a Jensen Interceptor III, a 1948 Mercury Convertible, a '55 Ford Thunderbird, a couple of Mercedes 300SL's, a half dozen Ferraris, a Maserati Sebring, an AC Ace Bristol and two Cobras, two Porsche 356's and three Corvettes among others. At the dinner that evening, we found there were several couples with whom we connected right away, and there is joy in finding that camaraderie right off.

Monday morning, after a sumptuous Texas sized breakfast, we started off in a light rain in an easterly direction out of Austin. Within 30 minutes we had left the built up area and were in the eastern reaches of the pine forest that gives the area such a different character from the rest of Texas. In the middle of nowhere, there appeared our next checkpoint at the Central Texas Motor Museum with 85 cars. A wonderfully diverse collection, it contained early 1900's primitives to current racecars with Packard, Dusenberg and Cadillac represented from the thirties. Why someone would build such a museum near nothing at all is a mystery to me. I guess that's where he lived, so that's where he built.

The Elite was the smallest car on the rally, the next smallest being the 1600 cc Morgan. As such I was certain I would have to pedal really fast to keep up, and sometimes I did. But other times, the narrow roads through the hill country of Texas allowed me to set a pace the big powerful cars had difficulty keeping. On one stretch, through a state park, the roads were really only about a lane and a half wide with trees lining both sides and dipping and swaying through the forest. While smooth, the road was not really grippy asphalt. In other words, just meant for an Elite! With a 427 Cobra in front of us, and a 427 Corvette behind, we felt like the meat in a hamburger, with someone asking "where's the beef?" By the end of the 25 mile section, we had nipped at the heels of the Cobra so much the he pulled over at a view point to let us by, while the Corvette had disappeared from our mirrors altogether. At the bar that evening, the Vette driver kept asking in amazement, "How does that little thing corner so well on those little motorcycle tires?" "When I was behind you I just couldn't get over how that thing looked like it was on tiptoes, but I had to drive like hell to keep up. Amazing!" I allowed as how the guy that designed it, Colin Chapman, had some pretty good ideas about this sort of thing.

As we headed west, we crossed I-35 near Kyle, TX. The crossing changed the nature of the land as well. It always amazes me that man-made lines, like the straight boundaries that define state lines and even Interstate highways, despite arbitrariness, seem to demark changes in topography, flora and fauna. And that is what occurred here. We left the pine forests and entered what is affectionately called "The Texas Hill Country".

The Hill Country of Texas is an area of limestone which has been cut through with several rivers, the Llano, Pedernales, Medina and the Guadalupe. The Guadalupe is the most prominent and one that we crossed and followed frequently. Hill Country is dry with mostly scrub oak and low plants that are drought tolerant. It is mostly empty country with big ranches that reach 35,000 acres in size, (about 55 square miles) and smooth roads that follow the contours and dips of the river cuts, yet have little traffic. So now you have the setting for 38 vintage cars with eager drivers. Nirvana!

There seems to be a natural rhythm for the various participants and frequently we ran in a group with several of the same cars: A 1956 Austin Healey 100 M and a 1955 100 S; a Mercedes SL; a Morgan 4/4 and several Ferrari's of various sizes from a 400 Superfast to a 250 GT, and two Cobra 427's . Sometimes it isn't the capacity of the car that matters but the heavy foot of the owner to exploit it. Clearly we were pedaling harder than most.

That night we went to "Canyon of the Eagles", a 940 acre park with numerous "luxury rustic" cabins surrounding the architecturally distinguished main lodge that overlooks Lake Buchanan. Pristine in its setting it was quite rustic yet well-staffed, comfortable and with marvelous food. Canyon of the Eagles is one of our favorite places we've ever stayed. After a wonderful lake cruise on Buchanan all the way to Marble Falls (where the captain put the bow of the boat directly under the falls for us), and a wonderful dinner, we had yet another treat. It seems that the absence of development in the area and the high clear air are ideal for viewing the stars. As a result the lodge has allowed an amateur astronomy club to set up their 15" and 17" reflecting telescopes on the premises. What a treat. We were able to see Mars at the closest it has been for centuries and stars millions of light years away quite clearly.

Waking early, we were anxious to get on the road again. Another monster breakfast and we left right behind Jimmy Dobbs in his Lancia Stratos with real rally history. Shortly after we left the flag point we lost the Stratos, as he was flying along the route. An hour later, the day was done for Jimmy. It seems he was passing through a narrow fence opening on a private ranch road when a fellow in an old truck towing a stock trailer going through the other way turned away from him to give more space and the rear of the trailer swung into Jimmy's left side at the rear wheel. The tire exploded and the suspension was severely damaged as well as a large gash opened in the side of the Stratos. One of the nice things about the Vintage Rallies organization is that they have two sweep trucks towing trailers with mechanics and tools. They will do their best to get the car back in the rally, and failing that, tow it back to home base. We were glad of that later!

With but a seven gallon gas tank, we were only able to make about 180 to 200 miles before filling. Not being aware that we were well out in the country, we were running on fumes when we came to a T intersection with a few buildings. It was the first civilization we had seen in quite a while but nothing that resembled a gas station. Our route instructions said left at the T, so we started out that way. After a few hundred yards, I saw nothing like fuel and decided to turn around, go past the T and see what was there. We were desperate. About a quarter mile back, around a bend was the most beautiful little country store with a gas pump. Several hunters were filling big trucks with 40 and 50 gallon tanks and I only hoped there would be enough left for us. There was, of course, and I learned a lesson. Out in the middle of the Hill Country, we learned to get gas when we passed through towns. There is a "whole lotta empty out there" as the locals say.

That evening we stayed at Horseshoe Bay on Lake LBJ. That is the lake named after President Lyndon Baines Johnson, but that's way too long so everyone calls it Lake LBJ. While cleaning the car with the hoses, towels and cleaners so thoughtfully provided by the rally folks, I noticed a leak from the engine area. Upon investigation I found that the rear carb was slightly leaking fuel from the seal where the float attaches to the bottom. It was just a seep and seemed to stop after a while. I was only concerned because the drip was directly above the exhaust manifold. Though there is a heat shield in between the drip and the hot exhaust, Lotus fiberglass has a reputation not unlike that of a Bic lighter when ignited, so I went to the mechanic's trailer and they agreed to look at it after everything was cool. Later, one pulled the carb apart and found the rubber seal with the shoulder at the bottom of the float attachment was badly deteriorated. They used some anaerobic sealant they promised would fix it until I could replace it. So Wednesday morning I started the car and watched as it warmed. Voila! NO LEAK! Well then, off to Mason and Mo Ranch.

We had driven about 25 miles to the town of Llano, (pronounced neither lahno, nor yahno, as I believed, but rather jahno!) where we came to a stop sign. As I slowed from highway speed (70-75 MPH) the throttle did not come back and the revs stayed at about 3000. So I switched off and stopped at the side of the road to see what was wrong. When I opened the bonnet, I found the front air cleaner cover was unbolted and it was askew. The throttle return spring had been attached to it so there was, in effect, no return spring. The nut was sitting at the bottom of the engine compartment so the repair was easy. I put the cover holding the spring back on its post and tightened the nut. It had apparently not been adequately tightened. But the bad news was that the rear carb seal was now leaking severely…far worse than before the attempted repair. With the reputation for Elite Flambé that I mentioned, I was of no mind to continue with fuel literally pouring onto the heat shield and exhaust.

Since I carry the two most important Lotus repair tools with me at all times (cell phone and credit card), I placed a call to the organizer, Rich Taylor, who, miraculously, answered. No problem says he, the sweep truck will be there in 30 minutes or less. I told him I had remembered Bill Parks in the Healey 100M carried an SU repair kit with him and asked if it would be possible to catch Bill at the next checkpoint in Mason and borrow the seal for a real repair. Rich said the fellow manning the check point had no phone. "Wait a minute", he said, "I have an idea". So we waited. Well over a minute as it turned out. The sweep truck came before the call and we loaded the Elite into the trailer in exchange for a Chevrolet Monte Carlo of recent rent-a-car vintage. Despite its rally sounding name, it was a living room couch with wheels. Nonetheless, it did have a stereo radio and air conditioning and it did run without a gas leak, unlike the Elite. So we headed to Mason. Rich called back and said he thought the message had gotten to the check point in time, but wouldn't know until we got there to see what we would find.

Mason is a lovely town of perhaps 5,000 with a town square around the courthouse as many old western towns are laid out. Around the square we found the check point and after the confusion of why someone in a modern Chevrolet Monte Carlo would stop at a Vintage Rallies check point, we were cleared. It seems Rich's idea was to call a Mason Realtor where he had a contact, dictate a note outlining the commandeering of the SU kit, have the Realtor lady hand carry it to Iain at the check point and then pray.

Once again I am reminded that those of us who drive old Lotuses are always potentially at the mercy of goodhearted strangers. And, usually, they prevail. It turns out we found the SU repair kit had indeed been left by Bill. The good Lord looks out for drunks and fools. I have been accused of being both with justification, and I appreciate the oversight.

Within another 20 minutes, the repair was accomplished, the leak was staunched, and we traded the Chevy for our Elite. We drove confidently off and immediately missed a turn, thereby heading the wrong way. Even more problematic, the sweep truck with the three car trailer was following our lead. After a half mile or so, when the next instruction made it obvious that we were clearly wrong, we made a U turn. That evening we learned that the sweep truck had to go another few miles to find enough room to turn around. Poor guys. After saving our rally, this is how they get treated!

We were anxious to make up for the maximum penalty of 500 points we had acquired at the Mason point so, when the road opened up to be a smooth, straight, wide line to the horizon, and Mukesh Bhatia blasted by in his Ferrari at about 125 MPH, providing a much more tasty morsel for Sheriff Buford T. Justice, I decided to see what our Elite was capable of for a top speed. She accelerated smoothly through an indicated 100 MPH but then seemed to run more roughly and struggle to do much more. After some distance she crept up to about 112, but didn't seem happy about it, so I eased back to about 5,000 rpm or a little over 80 MPH. From that point on, I noticed a lack of power and a roughness though all the gauge readings were normal.

We made it to the lunch check point just in time, and ate quickly as we were still behind. As at each stop, I checked the car generally, and the oil level specifically, and found it over a quart down. This was well above the normal quart per 250 miles rate that I had been experiencing prior to our top speed attempt. So I topped up and on we went. The next stop it was down again and that night I found it down another quart. Three quarts used in 260 miles. Everything was clean in the engine bay, no smoke to speak of was visible on deceleration, and yet the oil was going at a prodigious rate! I had already used the last of the four quarts I brought along. Worse yet I use Mobil 1, which is not only expensive but not readily available at the rural general store gas stops we frequented. So along with the route markers, we began looking for a place to buy oil in the larger (Pop.3,500 and up) towns. After 5 unsuccessful sorties, I finally sourced six quarts from a little NAPA store that mostly serves ranch equipment and GM small blocks. Cleaned 'em out, too, but at least I was certain I now had enough to finish the rally, so on we went.

The YO ranch resort is the last remaining remnant of a 55,000 acre spread that was pissed away by four generations, the last of whom built this very nice hotel resort in the small town of Kerrville, TX, about 20 miles from the original ranch. While a very nice place, it apparently is losing money and will be sold to a more competent operator soon. What was the largest ranch in Texas, and widely respected as well, will exist in name only having died with not a bang but a whimper.

We had a wonderful prime rib dinner and were then treated to the stories and artifacts of a world class collector of automobilia, Jacques Grelly.

Jacques has been associated with Le Mans since the early 1950's , even racing there several times, and has photos and posters from the earliest days of racing around the turn of the century(…the last one) through the present. Of course, there was a story accompanying each, including the fascinating story of the hostage taking of Juan Manuel Fangio by Castro sympathizers during the 1958 GP of Cuba. He was returned unharmed the day following the GP, but missed the race. This caused a great stir around the world as well as Cuba and gave credibility to the Castro rebels. It's amazing what we learned on this adventure.

Ultimately, I had to find more oil as the supply I thought would last to the end didn't. I used all I bought within the next day. I searched and found some at a Wal-Mart in Fredericksburg. By the finish, the Elite used 14 quarts of Mobil 1 at an average price (Wal-Mart low at $4.45 to NAPA high at $7.25) that made the cost of oil for the 1,065 miles of the rally higher than the cost of gas! We averaged 28.4 MPG for the trip even driving hard all the way, so if our oil consumption had been normal, it would have been an economical trip. After returning home, my mechanic Tom did a leakdown test and discovered a 45% leakdown in cylinder three and somewhat less in cylinder two. We surmise a broken ring or two which pressurized the crankcase and literally pushed the oil out the overflow on the fill tube. The bottom of the car was covered with oil and that supports this diagnosis. Still, the Elite ran to the finish and drove onto the trailer under her own power. Still looked the prettiest of all the cars as well!

The last day, Thursday found us crisscrossing the Guadalupe River all day, following its twists and turns for a while then rising to the top of a bluff to overlook the whole valley and then dive back to the river bed. What a delightful day. It was the coldest day of the trip at about 55 degrees Fahrenheit, and we were glad to be snug in our little coupe' as we watched the folks in open cars shivering despite bundling up thoroughly. The organizers told us to watch for "squeakers" which they defined as places where the passenger was likely to let out an utterance, based on fear, which sounded like a squeak. What we found instead was an "Oh, Sh!t!!" Ann, my stalwart navigator was looking down at the route notes as I approached a 90 degree left a "bit" too fast, because it also dropped about four feet so the occasional storm would run over it and she looked up to see nothing but barbed wire and cows straight ahead.. The Elite dropped like an elevator with a broken cable, crunching down on the bump stops. Meanwhile, I was still trying to turn left. Made it, too, but at the cost of a new expression from the right seat that was not in the manual. Maybe we can call it an "Annie"

The best part of the run that day, and perhaps of the whole rally, was the almost Stelvio like ascent to the top of a bluff, albeit compressed to $1/10^{th}$ scale, hairpin turns coming every 100-200 Yards. I was following Bill in the Healey 100 M and staying close but not catching him. Besides, I was afraid we would be gored by the six foot wide set of Texas Longhorns tied to the rear of his Healey, although they looked far more likely to slip forward and gore his wife Sandy in the navigator seat. There is no replacement for displacement, as they say. Besides, I had broken rings or I would have caught him. That's my story and I'm sticking to it!

When we finished the drive and were back at the Driskill, we had a chance to reflect with our new friends about the fun we'd had and the best vintage spirit we saw displayed.

Our hero of the trip was with us that day, Lindsey Parsons in a 1952 Allard J2-X. He never put ANY weather gear on the car, drove it flat out roaring like a wild beast as he passed. But that's not the only reason he is our hero. Despite being well into his seventies and having a prosthesis for one leg, he drove the car 1,500 miles from New Jersey to Texas and back home again after the rally just as he drove the rally! When I asked him why he wouldn't trailer it as all the rest had, he said "I want to go balls out as long as I can...that's how I keep young!"

Well, I submit that there's the answer to the question our friend Jim asked me, "What kind of idiot would drive a thousand miles...." a vibrant, alive, energetic, role model. And moreover, I hope to be asked that, frequently, when I am well into <u>my</u> seventies.

7 COMING HOME

My original plan was to drive some 2,600 miles with a group of about 55 Lotus Seven type vehicles on the USA 2005 tour from Houston to San Francisco, but it was not to be. My 1968 Lotus Seven needed repair after 2,300 miles, holing a piston from running too hard at Willow Springs Raceway. I struggled into Tehachapi, CA, spewing oil at a rate that would embarrass the Exxon Valdez. The Lotus was towed the rest of the way to the finish in San Francisco, and then to Woody Harris' shop in Vacaville, CA for an engine rebuild. After suitable time and a generous application of money, the car was pronounced fit to travel under its own power home to Colorado. Knowing mountain weather, I had arranged with a friend and fellow Lotus owner Bill Roushey to tow my trailer to a point west of the Rockies until I joined him west of the potential bad weather. I had the perfect plan! Remember, Grasshopper, hubris is always tested.

Starting out for home at 5:00PM on November 11, 2005 from Vacaville, CA, I quickly discovered several things about California drivers after edging my way on to I-80…They drive big SUV's & trucks with very bright lights that pierce down the neck of a Seven driver, and they drive them fast. I thought 80 was the route number, but it must be the suggested speed …in the slow lane. Never have I felt so small and disposable. I wouldn't have amounted to much more than a speed bump to most of these vehicles. But I soldiered on hugging the right lane with the hope that once past Sacramento, things would be better as I had planned a route over the Sierras on US 50, a lovely winding road through Lake Tahoe and into Carson City, NV. I would have made it fine, too, but for three things. First, the misunderstanding; second, the weather; and, finally, the belt.

The Misunderstanding: Since they had only finished the rebuild that day, one of the shop guys had gone for a test drive that, considering the 1350 mile trip on which I was about to embark, was a great idea. He said the gas gauge was on empty so he stopped to put in $5.00 worth and I thought I heard 5 gallons. At $3.29 a gallon that is a huge difference. I ran out of gas in the dark on the eastern part of Sacramento where the highway is 8 or 10 lanes wide, with no shoulder! Fortunately, I carry a spare gallon (since the gauge always reads empty), so I put it in with the cars and trucks whizzing by and made it to a gas station. After a refill of the spare gallon jug, the tank and the driver (20 oz. Coke and a giant Snickers bar) it was on the road again. That's when I met problem two.

The Weather: I had been a devoted student of the Weather Channel for about two weeks as I confirmed the dates for the trip and was pleased to note a high pressure dome was resting over the whole southwest for the weekend of my trip. As is often the case with western weather, local conditions belie the forecast and do as they please. Climbing the western slope of the Sierras I encountered a light mist. It wasn't really too bad until I got to Placerville where it started coming over the windscreen and I simply couldn't see. I saw a small motel where the kindly innkeeper allowed me to park under the registration portico - the only cover around. The temp had fallen to about 40 degrees and the motel room managed to get to about 60 with the puny wall heater available, so I tucked in with the idea of an early start and a big day. I awoke before first light, shivering. I decided to get a jump on the day, dressed with every layer I could summon and opened the door to …Snow.

At this point, the choice was to press on regardless, or call Bill and abandon the plan. As I have said before, God protects drunks and fools and I clearly wasn't drunk! Press On! The good news was that the sun came out and the road was dry within a few miles, it had been a little local system. On the other hand, as I climbed in altitude, it definitely got colder. And colder. And colder. By the time I got to the summit at 7,735 feet above sea level, it was about 16 degrees and I was getting stiff hands that could barely grip the wheel. So I stopped in South Lake Tahoe at the most wonderful International House of Pancakes just after 7:00 AM. They had just opened. The entire staff came out to look at this tiny car with the bundled up fool once they gave me a huge mug of hot tea to wrap my hands around. Of course, after my two course Coke and Snicker dinner I was starved. Believing that loading up on calories would keep me warm, I had a huge breakfast. Finally, fully filled and thawed, I rebundled and went out to the car. The waitress came out with a camera to document the stupidity of some car crazy subset of the human species.

Holding my head as high as I dared while keeping it out of the wind, I pressed on to the downhill run to Carson City. In the next hour I lost about 3,000 feet of elevation and gained about 30 degrees of temperature. Ahhh! One state down, three more to go.

Nevada. The empty West. The part of US 50 which is officially called (you can look it up) "The Loneliest Road in America" It is a beautiful two lane highway in perfect condition that runs roughly east/west across the center of Nevada and has none of the I-80 truck traffic that is so nerve wracking in a Seven. There are about a dozen little ranges of "mountains" that run in parallel fashion, north/south across the state. US 50 runs straight as a string across the valley floors between these ranges and then wiggles up and over to the next valley floor then straight til the next wiggle…an absolutely perfect sports car road except for one thing. It is "The Loneliest Road in America"

Once you leave Fallon at the western edge of Nevada until you reach Ely in the Eastern part of Nevada, a distance of 256 miles, there are only two towns with any services at all: Austin and Eureka. Fallon to Austin is about 110 miles, another 75 or so to Eureka and then 73 more to Ely. In between these points is a whole lot of empty! No gas, no food, people, or cell phone service, and almost no traffic. One vehicle every half hour is typical, and sometimes one can go an hour without seeing any other traffic. No worry for me though, I have a new motor and a PLAN. Again hubris is tested by problem three.

The Belt. Somewhere between Austin and Eureka, on a flat straight highway that I could clearly see five miles in either direction, the charging light on the dash panel lit up. What could be up, I thought, that the system isn't charging? So I began slowing and prepared to pull off to the shoulder although I could have parked in the middle of the highway with no concern of being hit. As I eased to a stop I noticed the temp gauge rising rapidly. Aha! Fan belt! No water circulation from the belt driven pump would do that. So, off with the bonnet and nose cone to have a look. There was the culprit, a loose bolt in the generator bracket, and the generator lying on its side. Apparently, the bolt in the front bracket hadn't been full tightened and backed out from the vibration at some point. The poorly supported generator had broken the back plate and the fan belt was thrown. But when? And where?

It could have been a quarter mile or two miles back. And even if I found the belt, the broken bracket wouldn't support the generator. And there wasn't a soul around; just the wind, the sky and the road. "The Loneliest Road in America".

There are times when we really want some solitude and quiet, yet we cannot find it in our hustle bustle world. Then there are times when the most beautiful thing we could have is a friendly face for support. This was one of those times. And yet, there was nothing. No sound. No sign of human habitation. No cell reception. I was totally, completely, fully alone. If I were to get out of here, I was going to have to figure it out.

I summoned up my best MacGyver attitude and went to search for something to turn into a suitable fan belt. Now, there isn't much room for spares in a Seven, so pickings were slim. I had a small tool kit with some wire and hose, spare clothing, and my gas jug, all tied down with bungee cords. YES, that's it, a bungee cord! I found one that looked to be a bit short, figuring that it would stretch, and began taking off the wire hook ends. Prying them off with a screwdriver and small pair of pliers took the better part of 30 minutes. Then I had to wire the ends together with my fine wire, like a bungee surgeon, which took another 15. During this time, not one vehicle passed.

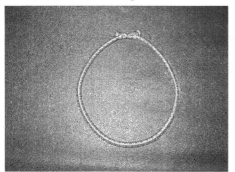 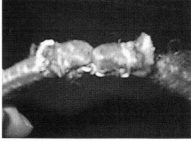

Bungee Belt, left and the surgical joint in detail on the right side

Finally, I had what looked somewhat like a fan belt. Green, puny and stretchy, maybe, but it was a beautiful fan belt to me. I slipped it over the crank and water pump pulleys, bypassing the generator. I figured I could make it quite a way without draining the battery and I knew Bill was within 350 miles. I started the car and it worked! It turned the water pump. I let the car tick over for a few minutes and the temp stayed steady. Eureka!

Yes that was my destination, but I wasn't sure how far it was. 20 miles? 40 miles? 60 miles? Well, I'd better button this up and get going. But before that, I thought I'd rev it a few times to make sure I had a solution that really worked. I flipped the throttle and the bungee flew. Well, I thought, the load of the water pump could have stretched one side and allowed the other to come off. I remounted the belt and this time I'd just ease the throttle up smoothly and gently. It worked perfectly until about 1,700 rpm. Each time I got to that speed the bungee would fly off. So I set off for Eureka at 1,600 rpm. First, second, third gear and we were moving. It worked fine. In fourth gear I was moving at about 24 miles per hour. Eight times as fast as the pioneers, yet still slow enough to see the varied scenery of central Nevada up close, and about a third the speed of the cars that passed.

In the nearly one hour drive to Eureka, one car passed me in the same direction at about 80 and two went by the other way. I had plenty of time to reflect on the place around me and I thought of the pioneers who had no road at all. As lost and alone as I felt, it was nothing compared to their situation. They were brave folks indeed. All this reflection was accompanied by the reassuring click, click, click of the bungee fan belt as it spun merrily around and the wire touched each pulley. As long as I heard that reassuring sound, all was well. Finally I reached the booming metropolis of Eureka, Nevada, Population 600. As this was a Saturday about 3:00 PM, much of the commercial part of Eureka was closed for the weekend, but the fellow at the gas station said the hardware store was open and maybe they could help. So I clicked up Main Street to the hardware emporium. The very kindly lady who owned the store asked what I needed. I said, "A fan belt for a 1968 Lotus Seven". I may as well have asked for a Flux Capacitor for my DeLorean.

She said she had lots of belts if I could just tell her what size I needed. So I got a length of wire rope and went out to measure. Taking off the bonnet and nose again, I rolled one front wheel up on the curb to get a bit more working room, and carefully wrapped the wire rope around both pulleys and marked the overlap spot with my pinched thumb and finger. Into the store I marched, where we found a matching size Gates belt for a washing machine. Nothing ventured, nothing gained they say so out to the waiting car I went. It was a struggle to get the belt over the flange on the crank pulley so I put the car into fourth gear and gently rocked it forward. On popped the belt. As I checked for fit, I found a perfect half inch of deflection...neither too loose nor too tight.

It was now after 3:30 and I had a long way to Richfield, Utah. Without a generator, I would need to follow the Lucas mantra for certain; Be home before dark! There was no way I could make that, and Eureka had cell signal, so I took a chance and called Bill. As is the case in much of any successful outcome, I was lucky. I reached Bill as he was checking into the motel in Richfield. He hadn't even taken his things up yet, and happily said he would head west with the trailer immediately. My mission was clear, drive as fast as possible toward Bill. Every mile I made would be two less for him...one west and another retracing east.

I drove with utter abandon; faster than I had since Willow Springs, disregarding the break in rules for the motor. I drifted around the curves in the wiggle parts and flew at a varying but high rpm on the flats. I made the 73 mile trip to Ely in less than an hour, wiggles included, and stopped for gas and to phone Bill. I had a message from him saying he had passed Delta Utah and was rolling west on 50. I left a message for him saying I was headed east from Ely toward Utah. It was now past 4:30 and the light was getting dimmer. The sun goes behind the hills and though it isn't "dark" it is "darker". I replaced my sunglasses with clear goggles and zipped my jacket and hood tightly before setting off. Again I flew toward the east without lights, but with the benefit of a full moon and a clear sky. As there was almost no traffic, I was doing quite well.

When an occasional vehicle would appear, I could see them for miles before they were near and I would ease over to the right shoulder to give plenty of room. I was tempted to turn my lights on, but was more concerned about running out of battery than I was of seeing and being seen. That was almost my undoing. After another 30 or 40 minutes in what was now full darkness, I saw an approaching vehicle and eased over to the right.

As he passed, I realized it was Bill with the trailer who was now flying *away* from me. I hit the brakes and pumped them to make the brake lights flash, preparing to turn around and begin the chase. Just as I slowed enough to make the turn, I saw all of Bill's brake lights on the Range Rover and the trailer light up the evening sky in the most beautiful display of red imaginable. Bill had come about 185 miles west and I had gone about 150 east. We got the Seven secured on the trailer and headed for Richfield.

Sunday morning we headed off to Denver with a clear weather report and the Seven safe and secure on the trailer. We cruised smoothly east to about Rifle CO where we began to encounter rain. By the time we got to Glenwood Springs, it was turning to snow. When we passed Vail, we were in the thick of an unforecast, full blown, winter storm, with 10 to 12 inches expected and winds too. Trucks were chaining up and on the pass several were jackknifed and had slid off the road. Bill was as steady as a rock and we slowly made it over the top.

The conditions were bad all the way to the tunnel but gradually got better as we came down the eastern slope toward Denver. We stopped for a break in Downieville and took the attached picture. As Buzz Bilsberry said, "Why has he sprayed his car with expanding foam? Does it help keep the snow out or something?"

The Seven on the trailer after crossing Vail Pass in the storm

Every trip I have taken in the Seven has been memorable, unlike the dozens I have taken in a "real" car. I think that is what keeps me setting off on these boondoggles; the sense that getting there is not a foregone conclusion. It is a voluntary bit of welcome adventure in a too regular and regulated world, I guess. And, besides, how many stories would be worth writing about driving a Minivan across Interstate 80?

8 A PILGRIM GOES TO LOTUS

Now I understand. I finally get why English cars are designed the way they are. I get why the people are so stoic with a wry humor, and why Lotus commands such fierce loyalty.

As with all stories, this one starts much earlier to reach these not very startling conclusions. I have always had affection for things British beginning with the Terry Thomas film "School for Scoundrels" in the late '50's. There is a resilience and humor there in the face of discomfort that is very appealing. Then came the Bond films, and who of us didn't want to be "Bond, James Bond"; so suave and resourceful in the high stakes games of love and spying. And, finally, the music: The Beatles, Rolling Stones, Kinks and the Dave Clark Five, among others, accompanied our passage into adulthood. But the thing that really defined the British culture to me was the cars; specifically sports cars. While my Dad had a Buick Roadmaster (a straight eight with a Dynaflow transmission), there were these really cool, dashing sports cars that could run rings around that Buick. And coolest of all of them was Lotus. So small, yet perfectly formed; light and lithe yet able to run with a Corvette. I was hooked.

Yet dreams and reality frequently diverge, and while the dream may have been dormant it never went away. I bought practical cars, usually used, instead of "them furrin' jobs" after my Dad bought a Fiat 600 as an experiment in economy and I learned to my dismay about trailing throttle oversteer one slick, rainy night. Finally, after raising a family and getting the mortgage down to a reasonable level, it was my turn. After learning a fair bit of race craft in an Austin Healey Sprite, and finding that I had reached its limits, I bought my vintage racing Elan and began to learn what makes a Lotus so special.

The DNA starts with Colin Chapman. First is his training in aircraft structures. He was a pragmatic and solution oriented engineer, who reasoned that the less weight one had to accelerate, slow and turn, the easier would be the solution. So, the mantra of "Add Lightness" was born. He found delight in exploiting a gap in the rules, or in proving the "experts" wrong. Frequently he took a concept that had been abandoned as unworkable and made it work. Then he attracted like-minded people to not only work for him but to do impossible things under his encouragement and, occasionally, his hectoring. All Lotus cars share these elements. Unlike Porsche who has massaged their original concept and polished it to perfection, or Ferrari who always built the car in support of the engine, Lotus has always tried new approaches to solve the problem. Look at the amazing variety of presentation of just the road cars: Front engine, mid-engine, FWD, RWD, two seat, four seat, Aluminum, Steel, Fiberglass, carbon fiber, space frame, a monocoque (fiberglass, no less) sheet metal backbone, extruded and glued aluminum beams; the mind boggles.

I have been captured heart and soul by the character of these mechanical devices. In fact it is the notion that these inanimate things have character that captivates. They are a widely disparate lot, yet all have a familiar energy about them. A "Lotusness"

As I learned more, I became anxious to experience the different personalities of the wide variety of cars called Lotus. Now I have nine, and they each have different things that endear them to me. For high speed touring on Interstate and primary roads, the Turbo Esprit is in its element. In town, or for an effortless errand on a mild day, the M100 Elan fits the bill. For Canyon carving, either the Seven or Elan is the choice, depending on my mood. For general "Road Dancing" the ballerina is the Elite, and the distance champ is the Europa Special. If we want to get away for a weekend with the variety of gear we take, then the Plus 2 is perfect. On the track, it is either the Elan or Eleven, depending on the nature of the competition.

Finally, comes the wish to make a pilgrimage to the source of the energy – to feel the ghosts and bridge the years. So this past August, Ann and I went to England to visit friends made through the Lotus connection, to visit the factory as well as Classic Team Lotus in Norwich, and finally to experience the past at the Goodwood Revival.

We were warmly welcomed by kindred spirits who I had met on the USA 2005 tour (where more than 50 mad dogs and Englishmen toured from Houston to San Francisco in Sevens) and got to drive three different Lotus Sevens on their home turf. The narrow hedge lined lanes that rise and dip over the countryside through quaint villages, careen through roundabouts and present slow moving farm obstacles, absolutely demand a car that can squirt, handle and brake. In other words, a Lotus Seven. I don't think we ever got above 70 and we never stopped fully, we just danced along through the countryside for miles. No wonder there is no pressure for cup holders, stereos and auto transmissions… they would simply dim the experience. No wonder the cars are small and maneuverable …no Buick would fit down the lane and, if it did, it would be exhausting to drive. And no wonder they top out at 75 MPH or so…one cannot go any faster. It is as if Darwin's law applied to motorcars; these are perfectly suited to their intended purpose.

Then we went to Hethel to see the heritage of Lotus racing at Classic Team Lotus. Clive Chapman and his team welcomed us with open arms and shared the spirit of those race teams past as they busily prepared three cars for Goodwood. One of the people who was there then and still carries the effort forward is Bob Dance. His charges included Jim Clark, Graham Hill, Jochen Rindt and Mario Andretti and each won a Lotus F1 world championship. Now he prepares cars like the Type 21 that was the first GP winner ever for Team Lotus, the type 32 that Jim Clark used to win his Tasman Series Championship, and the type 99 that Ayrton Senna won the last ever GP for Team Lotus. He is a walking history of Lotus Formula One, and a charming and gracious man. Lunch with Clive at the Bird in Hand, the pub that has seen 40 years of Lotus history itself, was the perfect bow on the visit. There is an enduring quality to these places. Nothing here is "modern". Rather, there is a respect for the craft and doing it right. They don't remodel to keep up with the Joneses; they adapt and reuse what is there. They understand history and preserve and protect it, never turning their backs on where they have come from in a rush to get where they are going. This 'steadiness" is why there will always be an England.

So how does this translate into letting Lotus compete as a manufacturer of contemporary cars in a world market? We went a few hundred yards down Potash Lane to find out.

At first blush, the home of Lotus doesn't seem to be a manufacturing facility, but a research facility. It's quiet outside with none of the noise, bustle and transporters leaving one would expect at an auto plant. I have visited Ford and GM plants and the contrast is enormous. The throughput in one of those plants is greater per hour than this one in a week and each reflects that. There is sort of an unspoken pride that Lotus still hand builds each car, using the most innovative materials and design.

The plant is really more assembly than manufacturing.. Components and sub-assemblies arrive from various parts of the common market and are installed by a dedicated crew who look to be building a Tamiya model in 1 to 1 scale. Complete front and rear moldings are affixed to the bonded chassis that has already had its sub-assemblies like suspension and brakes attached. Every car is hand painted by a human being – no paint robotics for Lotus! And each car goes on a rolling road and through a high pressure water test displaying a new level of quality control for this company. What is evident throughout, is a pride and dedication to the brand. These people are energized by the fact that it is a Lotus they are producing. The test track just outside the factory door is a distinction that documents the way things are at Lotus, and a reason for the pride. There are three type 119 gravity race winners from the Festival of Speed that are displayed in the entry. No other car company has beaten Lotus there.

Having seen the source, Ann and I headed for Goodwood to see the early Lotuses in their period context. If you ever get the chance, go to the Goodwood Revival. Words cannot convey the scope and intensity of this "Happening". While the Monterey Historics are wonderful, and big show at Road America has more Can-Am thunder than I've ever seen, they pale next to the Revival. Not one famous driver but a dozen, not five championship winning cars but fifty, and not millions of dollars' of nostalgia, but hundreds of millions. Meanwhile, overhead are Spitfires and P51 Mustangs flying in formation; so close you can almost touch them. Lord March's estate is 12,000 acres and is magnificent. The fans are informed and show up regardless of weather - keeping a smile and a wry comment ready while watching attentively even in the face of rain and what were literally gale force winds. The racing is fierce in every run group; cars you've only seen in magazines are thrashed, slid and revved in the sun and rain equally. Almost every run group had Lotus cars and they were always competitive. As I wandered through the paddock, I saw the evolution of race technology exemplified with the Lotus cars frequently showing some innovation a year or two earlier than others. There is high regard for the Lotus brand throughout the paddock, along with the famous men who have Lotus connections: Stirling Moss, Jackie Stewart, and others. It was a Lotus and automobile and aircraft overload!

So, now, I understand. And, what is more, I appreciate the Lotus heritage that runs from that first Austin Seven based trials car to the latest Evora and the future Lotus cars. It's in their DNA. And, maybe, in mine, too.

9 THE LEAD SLED RULES

My friend John is a really good guy. I only mention this because he doesn't deserve what befell him in finding his dream car-a Lead Sled Mercury like James Dean drove. He has lusted after a '50 Mercury two door for a long time, keeping track of cars offered for sale, cars sold, and their sales prices. After several years and lots of auction cars he'd seen, John decided it was time to get off the sidelines and make his move.

As a complete stranger to eBay John asked me for some help. I, of course, am a veteran of the medium with hundreds of transactions. The stack of kitsch I have been able to acquire is the envy of every garage saleista in the country. In the course of these varied transactions I have made every mistake it is possible to make. Some should have been impossible but I still made them. Fortunately, most of them were made on relatively low cost transactions so the tuition cost was manageable, although if one adds the enormous embarrassment cost, it is off the charts. So, in May on a road trip from Denver to the Mecum auction in Indianapolis I began the "Old Car" tutorial with John, starting with the perfect road snack. I was introduced to this delicacy by Bill Howard who entrusted the recipe to me and I only pass it along to true "Car Guys". Take a can of Kraft Easy Cheese - bacon cheddar preferred, (I refer to this as hydraulic cheese for obvious reasons) and fill Frito's Scoops individually. Eat as many as possible for great satisfaction and a years' worth of cholesterol. As we pounded them down (with Cokes) across Kansas, I reiterated four ***ironclad rules*** for buying a car off the interweb.

Rule 1: *Know what you want. Exactly*. If you have the "itch" to get a collectible car, many attractive possibilities will present themselves. How will you know which one is right unless you are have in your own mind a mental picture of the car you want? That doesn't mean it cannot be purple when you "saw" it as red, but it does mean that a really cool '57 Chevy Bel Air is no substitute for a "50 Merc, nor is a 'Vette for a Lotus.

Rule 2: *Talk to the seller...several times.* I believe you can tell a lot from the owner about a car by "visiting", as they say in the south. If we begin with the premise that nobody needs a toy car, then there had better be some feeling of attachment from the seller. An owner who has loved his car is clearly different than one who has owned it for investment - guess which I prefer. How the owner talks about the car is almost tender if he has enjoyed it, and almost bitter if he hasn't. Guess which I prefer.

Rule 3: *Never offer to buy any car unless you have, or someone you trust completely has, inspected and driven personally.* Even if the person who inspects the car for you is not an expert in that make and model, he can make sure it starts easily, drives straight and doesn't smoke or stall. He can feel the steering and brakes and how it handles bumps and dips. He can listen for strange noises; unusual thumps, bangs, squeaks and buzzes. And, finally, no matter how many photos one has there is no substitute for a close up visual inspection of the car – over and under, engine and trunk, inside and out.

Rule 4: *Know what you are willing to spend for the car and don't get caught up in a bidding war.* On eBay, the safest way to do this is to place your maximum bid just about 15 seconds prior to the end of the auction unless you have a snipe bidding service. I prefer the knowledge that I have placed my own bid. Of course, I have lost a couple of auctions at the last second, yet I realize that someone has bid more than I was willing to spend and this can go on and on for hundreds or thousands of dollars. Hence the rule.

Basically these "rules" of mine are designed to protect me from myself. Finding a very cool car that is available to me is no less intoxicating than meeting a lovely girl who is. In both cases it is wise to move slowly in order to avoid making a fool of myself - or worse.

So, in the spirit of friendship I shared these "rules" with John. I also passed along a *Side Glances* column with Peter Egan's masterful advice on this same subject which is much more colorfully phrased and humorous than mine yet carries similar warnings. John listened and read. He even asked lots of clarifying questions. Then John acted.

Following all the rules but number three, John bought a car over the interweb from an eBay listing which had not sold. The trouble is that rule number three is far and away the most important. It is the linchpin of the decision to buy or not buy. It is the ***uber*** rule!

The car, the long sought after '50 Merc, was beautiful in the photos. A brilliant orange and purple with an airbrushed Marilyn Monroe on the trunk and James Dean and Elvis on the fender skirts, it was spectacular. Subtle? No, but just the thing to make an entrance at the local hot rod show and go cruising at the drive in. John fell in love and threw logic as far as that car was from him - Colorado to Tennessee.

John assured me that the seller, a dealer, had been driving the car so it had to be in good shape, right? And the dealer had only bought it because the guy who built it was in deep financial trouble after pouring his heart and savings into the car and needed money right away. If that is not a reassuring tale I don't know what is. See Rule number two. John figured since the "really nice" seller had been driving the car it must be just fine. I said I had a friend who could go look at the car within a week but John had the itchy trigger finger we get when emotions rule, so he declined.

By mid-May the deal was transacted and the car was shipped to an anxiously awaiting John. When it arrived ten days later it was, mostly, as described. The paint and bodywork were great. The engine was exactly as advertised. The workmanship on the interior and trim was strong. But, and this is a bigger but than J Lo has, the front suspension, transmission and brakes were each a disaster. The dealer's verbal buy back promise was immediately withdrawn and he was just like Sergeant Schultz, saying "I know nothing!" The net result was clear; an undrivable car.

While this was a bitter pill for John, he is a problem solver so he began the process to get the car right. The really hard part is that John's grandson who is developmentally disabled loves cars, especially colorful cars, and perhaps the largest part of John's motivation for getting this particular Merc, and the reason he pulled the trigger so fast, was to go out summer nights and get ice cream with his grandson. Dream delayed.

So I get a call from John for suggestions about who might get the car running again. I suggested a friend of mine, who said, "I don't do old anymore." John calls a collector car club and asks who is qualified to get this work done, gets referrals and starts calling. All are booked through the summer. Well that doesn't fit "The Dream", so John finds another guy makes long list of things that needed mechanics service, reviews the list with the mechanic on the phone to be sure this all fits his capability and is assured he is available to work on the car right away. He makes a clear typed list., delivers it and the car to him right away to start work, but finds after a couple of weeks nothing has been done.

He pulls the car from that guy and takes it to shop number two, sadly a referral from the first guy. This clown wants a $2,000 deposit for parts and John succumbs to the need to get the car on the road and gives it to him. As Julia Roberts says in Pretty Woman, "Big Mistake". Somehow this guy spends a few weeks and a bunch of the deposit while actually making the car worse. How much worse, John had no idea, but he decided he had to get the Merc out of there, and worry later about how to get his deposit (or some of it) back. This is where I come back in to the story. I got a call from John asking me to drive with him up to this guy's place in north Denver, offer moral support, then follow him to the third mechanic's place while he delivered the car, and then ride home with him. A "three hour road trip" he said. Of course he bribed me with a promise of Freddie's Frozen Custard if I said yes and would bring along the hydraulic cheese and scoops. Off we went.

Picking the car up was less confrontational that I had expected and I was anxious to make tracks, thus I was surprised when John, zigging and zagging, stopped after only a block or so. When I pulled up behind him on the shoulder of the highway, flashers on, he looked quite concerned and was a whiter shade of pale then even Procol Harum claimed.

"This blankety blank car is undrivable!!" he moaned "I can't drive this even the seven miles we have to go. I'm all over the road." I observed as how following him had been interesting with the swaying path he had taken, dipping right as a prelude to turning left. When I got down in front of the car to take I look I could see the problem immediately. The front wheels were toed out at a cartoon like angle – probably 15 degrees or more. No wonder the car yanked right, then left. The heading taken depended on which wheel had traction at the moment. And, the faster John went the worse it got. He proposed calling for a trailer. I countered with irrefutable logic – we were only going seven miles and, even driving slowly, would be done before a trailer could get where we were right then. "You can do this John", said I. "And I will be right behind you with the flashers on."

Press on! Staying to the right, on the shoulder whenever possible, and at a very slow pace, we finally made it to the third mechanic. His shop was down a long drive behind his residence, a drive that started between two brick pillars and meandered alongside to the shop out back. I held my breath as John lurched between those pillars nearly hitting both and wove two black streaks all the way down the drive. Hans, the mechanic waiting for the car to arrive stood there watching the whole thing, speechless.

John staggered out of the car soaking with sweat and asking for water. Hans decided that a tour of the shop along with a bottle of cold water would calm John down so we began walking through the projects in the shop. It was immediately apparent that Hans did good work as each of the cars in the place from an old '30's Ford to a mid '60's Mustang and his own Chevelle were on their way to or already had achieved gorgeous status. After seeing the equipment in the shop and what the guys could do with it, I felt that John had finally found a shop that would get the Merc on the road. Hans confirmed my feeling when he raised the car on the lift and began inspecting the front end alignment.

It was a Rube Goldbergian array of arms, levers, rods and pivots. Any motion initiated at the steering wheel had a half-dozen detours before it reached the wheels. And even if that all could be adjusted properly the suspension looked shot with worn springs shocks and old fashioned kingpins instead of ball joints. Finally, the guy had installed disc brakes on the rear axle but left the old drum brakes on the front. What a mess!

Hans shook his head disparagingly not knowing where to begin, I suspect. Finally he spoke, hesitantly at first, but with more energy the longer he went. The gist was this: "You can spend $2,500 getting the stuff that's here to work better or replace everything with a new sub-frame containing modern adjustable independent suspension, disc brakes and rack and pinion steering for about $4,000". There was a long protracted silence. John looked down and at me as if waiting for me to share my opinion. So, I asked if we could have a few minutes alone to talk. Hans and his helper turned to leave but John stopped them, saying anything I had to say could be said in front of them. I strongly supported the latter choice as I knew John wanted to take his grandson Zach for lots of drives and cruise in shows. The only real solution was total replacement. Another long silence.

Finally John spoke saying something about how he had felt the same way but needed to hear somebody else say it. At this point Hans told him that if the replacement was done he wouldn't hesitate to drive it at 80 all the way to Chicago. John said "Do it!" Hans said he would have the parts required and a preliminary budget by the next day. The next morning I got an email from John saying Hans had sent him the promised information and that John had ordered the parts on his credit card. He finally felt things were going his way. Hans had a supplier he used before who said it would take ten days to make the parts. John ordered from a second place because Hans was told by this supplier that the entire front assembly for that very application was in stock and would be there in a few days. Hans figured John would be driving in style in less than three weeks. Dream in sight!

Three weeks later…still no parts. John had been calling repeatedly and getting different people at the supplier none of whom knew what was going on. After reaching a manager John was assured that the entire assembly would be shipped in two days and would bolt right in. If there is ever a phrase to strike fear in the heart of a car guy, "bolt right in" is right up there with "You can't miss it" or "it's just like the original part but at half the cost". Ever hopeful and optimistic, John believed.

If you cannot guess what happened next, you are either a hopeless optimist or brand new to the world of project planning. The assembly came incomplete and unusable. Without going into graphic detail, there is a main cross member that supports the suspension and brakes. It didn't come close to fitting, even if lots of fabrication was done by Hans, far less being ready to "bolt in". John found himself at crossroads again.

Hans recommended John order from the first supplier, the one that he had used before but had to make the assembly. Of course, they *still* had to make it. So, another two weeks went by, but this time when the part came it was the right one. Hans and his guys went to work fitting and fabricating the new front end. As usual, it took lots of problem solving to make it all fit right but nothing too difficult this time. John called me thinking he saw the light at the end of the tunnel. Or was it another oncoming train?

Finally, as we neared the end of August with roughly three months of summer evenings long gone, John called to say that Hans was taking the car for alignment and it would be ready for pickup on Friday, giving a weekend full of promise for John and his grandson. Yet again, an obstacle arose. In testing, Hans had discovered a brake actuating problem – the brakes required extraordinary pedal pressure. After tracing it down to a too short pivot lever, Hans had fixed it by Monday and pronounced the car ready to drive! John called to ask if I would accompany him to pick up the car since I had been along for much of the ride so far. I was delighted to accept and on Tuesday, as we rode the 45 minutes or so to Hans' shop, I could see the mixed emotions roiling through my normally happy friend. He was hopeful that the car would meet his expectations, yet wary of getting his hopes up and even fearful of another impending disaster. He had come so far and made such an emotional investment; not to mention all the cash he had spent. Dream or Nightmare?

Well, as it turns out, Hans and his crew created a pretty nice dream. No, it is not perfect; it's still bottoming out of the rear springs with four aboard and the turn signals crapped out and the shifter is still balky. But boy oh boy does it run down the road nicely. I followed him home across a rural two lane highway and down Interstate 25 and the car was smooth and graceful with no hint of erratic behavior. More importantly, John was relaxed behind the wheel. And you should have seen the looks he got with people rubber necking all the way across five lanes. Wow!

The best part, the very best part, was that John took the car to his son's house and parked on the side street around the corner then went and got his grandson Zach. As John brought him around the corner, Zach bubbled over like a fountain at the Bellagio. He could barely contain the excitement he felt and that was before he went for a ride. John and his wife came over to our house afterward and all four of us went to Freddie's for burgers and custard. We had a ball feeling just like teenagers again. They even gave John his meal free for bringing such a cool car!

Based on the freeway reactions, plus those from Zach, the four of us, and Freddie's staff, I'd say the message is quite clear...The Lead Sled Rules!

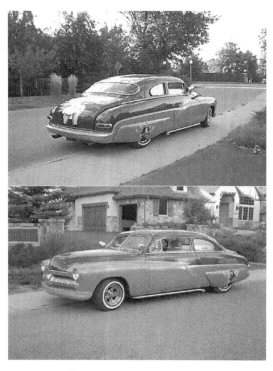

10 THE PRINCESS AND THE GNOME

Though this sounds like a fairy tale, it is not. "The Princess" is an name affectionately given to my Lotus Elite Type 14, by my wife Ann, who thinks all pets, including our cars, deserve a proper name. While I don't like to anthropomorphize any inanimate object, I know that to object to naming the Elite would risk hurt feelings with Ann, so "The Princess" it is. On the plus side, it is much better than our Esprit named "Lucy" or Plus 2 known as "Pooh Bear" (don't ask) so I guess I should be grateful.

In November 2003, we did the Texas 1000 in the Elite and though it finished the rally, it was badly wounded – broken rings in two cylinders – and needed some attention. Luckily, Ian Rainford, now another Elite owner and a knowledgeable Coventry Climax engine builder, lives not too far away. I asked Ian to rebuild the engine and he did a wonderful job…it is smooth and strong. So, after four and a half years and suitable break in miles, it was time for another adventure. We applied to the Copperstate 1000, a one thousand mile rally round the state of Arizona scheduled from April 5-9, 2008, and were accepted. We towed the Elite on an open trailer to Phoenix with eager anticipation.

Many of the vintage rallies have strict Time, Speed and Distance requirements, and some are little more than a high speed romp through fantastic scenery with a bunch of beautiful old cars. In fact, based on the enormous amount of food and drink at each stop, this category of rally has gained the nickname "Wheels to Meals"…a not unfair appellation. The Copperstate is one of these, but with some fairly restrictive application requirements resulting in a wide variety of over 70 wonderful cars from early pre-war Bentley Speed Sixes, a Hispano-Suiza and a Delahaye to 1960's Alfas, Ferraris, Maseratis, and Bizzarinis from Italy, a Facel Vega and Renault Alpine from France, Gullwing Mercedes, Porsches and BMWs from Germany, and Jaguar XKSS, C, and E types as well as a lovely Triumph TR2 from England. All these cars had provenance and big engines…at least two liters. There was only one car with less than a 1,300 cc engine and only one Lotus…The Princess.

Ross and Ann's Elite next to a Bizzarini GT and a Jaguar XK150FHC

Prior to starting the rally, we had occasion to have breakfast with a past coworker of Ann's at a Cracker Barrel restaurant. It seems they sell lots of memorabilia of really questionable taste at these places, and, of course, Ann spied a gnome for sale just like the one that my son and his girlfriend recently had had stolen from their garden. Their real gnome, named Gary (I told you everything gets named) may not have been returned, but we could take this Gary on an adventure, send ransom photos and return him to his rightful spot in the garden. I bought the gnome and we decided to take him to the kickoff party Saturday night.

Gary was not only a hit but took one too. He got dropped! It goes without saying that this was a tragedy of more than laughable proportions. It wasn't pretty picking up pieces of Gary, and we transported his face piece back to the trophy case in memoriam. Of course he had to be replaced so early Sunday morning I returned to the Cracker Barrel and bought two more gnomes…just in case.

Throughout the trip Gary was handed off, as though he were chattel, from car to car and escaped without a scratch. Yet one night of irresponsible partying and just look at his fate. Let this be a lesson to all of us who are over served while indulging in a carefree manner!

Starting from Diablo Stadium in Phoenix at one minute intervals beginning 10:00 Sunday morning, the Princess, wearing number 14 of course, was staged about mid pack and left around 10:30. Through the surface streets of Phoenix we drove sedately until we reached open highway about 15 minutes from the stadium. Rolling along with this mobile classic auto show was a treat. We passed a few cars and were passed by quite a few as we climbed from near sea level in Phoenix to nearly 6,000 feet for our lunch stop just past Payson, AZ. We were driving wide sweeping curves on a four lane highway as we changed from desert to alpine climate, and the Princess handled it with dignity if not real gusto. She could keep a 70-75 mph pace whether the road was winding or straight. Some of the stronger cars were faster on the straight sections though we'd catch or pass them in the winding portions. Water temp and oil pressure were perfect and we relaxed and just enjoyed the scenery. From saguaro to pine trees, it was ever changing - and getting cooler too. The ambient temperature went from around 85 degrees F to 65 – perfect for an Elite and her passengers. This is a very different Arizona from the one we all first recall. A terrain and climate very reminiscent of our home state of Colorado –of course we were in heaven!

At the lunch stop at the Chaparral Pines ranch east of Payson, we enjoyed a tasty barbeque and were besieged with requests to let Gary ride in various cars. Well, as trusting guardians we, of course, allowed him to ride with any and everyone who asked. This made him subject to all sorts of indignities, which propriety won't permit me to disclose. As a consequence, the motor cycle mounted Highway Patrol escorting us was forced to take him for rehabilitation at the conclusion of the rally. But, I digress. Without worrying about Gary, we were able to stretch the legs of the Elite over the winding roads of lovely forested northeastern Arizona

In fact, we were leading a group of about five cars at a prodigious rate of speed when a local police officer, coming the other way, saw us and turned on his flashing lights and made a scary U turn to pursue

All of us slowed, of course, waiting for the inevitable. Then a funny thing happened. He cut off the car following me and stopped the rest of the group. I found out later that they had all gotten speeding tickets for going 85 in a 55 zone, even though the cop said he had clocked them at 93 or more. He didn't want to take them to jail which he would have had to do if they were ticketed for more than 30 over the limit. Why hadn't I been stopped, I wondered...I had been leading them after all.

In talking with our escort officers, it turns out that the Elite has a very small "Signature" on police radar from the front, due to the lack of metal frame or body and the sloping radiator, which limits the reflected signal, so the radar locked on to the big steel bodied Maserati following me. Who knew that Chapman was so prescient?

That was about the only bad part of the afternoon drive as the sky was a perfect cobalt blue, the temperature was in the mid 60's and the road was smooth, clear and winding. As we drove through the forest to our destination, The Greer Lodge Resort at Greer, we passed through cool little towns with names that had an intrigue of their own; Show Low, Pinetop, Lakeside and Hon-Dah, not Japanese at all but White Mountain Apache complete with a casino. The Greer Lodge is at the end of a road that goes nowhere but to the lodge and is thus a rustic but modern oasis in the middle of an alpine forest.

The road from Alpine to Morenci, AZ, retraces, on a shelf along the eastern spine of the Rockies, the path taken in 1540 AD by Coronado and his conquistadors to find the seven cities of Cibola which were supposedly laden with gold. Currently called the Coronado Trail or US 191, it was formerly known as Highway 666, or the Devil's Highway. We would know it's true nature soon enough.

Gary, of course, had learned nothing about proper behavior from his previous night's bash (quite literally) and was found flirting with the ladies and deep into the booze once again. Those of us who are more responsible than he, stuck to wine and cigars and were snug in bed with five or more hours of deep and restful sleep ahead of us until the six o'clock call to the cars for departure to the most winding and tricky road we would have during the entire 1,000 miles.

At Alpine, the last fuel for about 120 miles, everyone refueled. Of course, the normal clientele for the Alpine gas station is pickup trucks and an occasional tourist, so everyone came to see this parade of incredible cars. We refueled with 5.5 gallons making our mileage so far about 34 mpg. In fact we used only 28.7 gallons for the entire trip which is less than the Bentley took at this fill!

It is quite a good thing we filled up first as that beast took all but the dregs

On to the road. We started off from the gas station behind a '64 Corvette, a Triumph TR2 and the Bentley. The grade was fairly steep as we left Alpine and headed over the top of the Coronado Trail so we were hard pressed to keep up. After about five miles the road began to get really twisty and within a very short time we had caught the Corvette. We followed him for a while, falling behind in the straights and quickly catching him in the turns. After tolerating this for a bit, he finally waved us by and within about five turns had disappeared from our rear view mirrors. I thought of Stirling Moss' observation on driving his Elite home to London from Goodwood, "I averaged 65 miles per hour and never went over 70".

This little overachiever simply carries speed through the twisties so well it can stay with or even pass cars which are theoretically much faster. As you might imagine, both the Bentley and Triumph were dispatched in similar fashion. Then we had a wonderful road all to ourselves for about forty miles. Short chutes followed by hairpins alternating with sweepers both up and down hill for forty miles can really work up an appetite. Fortunately, we were welcomed at a little rest stop on a point overlooking the valley. What a delight to relive the road, while stretching and having a snack, with those who had just conquered it.

From the rest stop we continued in like fashion for another 30 miles or so and as the San Francisco river valley opened up approaching Morenci, we came to the biggest hole in the ground I have ever seen. The Morenci open pit copper mine is staggering in its scope; 60 square miles in surface area and almost a mile and a half deep, each day they remove 12,000,000 tons of earth to obtain 25 million pounds of copper. Copper on the world market is approaching $4 per pound, so that is $100,000,000 per day in copper revenue.

But the best part of all is that the trace amounts of other minerals they recover pay for the operating expense of the mine so the copper revenue is pure profit! As we observed the Terex trucks they use to move the ore from an overlook they looked like ants yet their tires are 12 feet tall and they carry hundreds of thousands of pounds of ore per trip.

As awe inspiring as this operation was, it signaled the end of the alpine environment as we spit out onto the desert floor. Just before we had descended though, we had one last "wow" moment following the Bentley around the last few hairpin corners. What a view!

While we calmly motored, Mike wrestled the Beastley around the corners

In each trip there is a best and worst segment. We had just finished the best and were headed for the worst. South to Interstate 10 and west to Tucson, for about 175 miles, we fought heat, wind, big trucks and boredom. The wind was blowing from the southwest at about 40 miles an hour with higher gusts, so both going south and west we fought a quartering wind. Ann and I put the side windows in on the windward side to cope, but nothing could help being tossed about like a potato chip in the gusts or each time we passed or were passed by an 18 wheeler. And of course the Elite is not in its element buzzing along at 5,000 plus rpm for almost three hours through the sagebrush.

Nonetheless we made it to the Starr Pass Resort in Tucson where we were to spend two nights. A magnificent facility, we felt like royalty in our luxury room and fully appointed bath. After a cooling shower and a change of clothes, we retired to the bar and patio for the evening. What was a hot day became a delightful evening and after the long dinner hour, we actually enjoyed the fire in the pit on the patio overlooking the twinkling lights of Tucson.

The following morning we prepared to ascend Mt. Lemmon, a climb from about 3,000 feet to the 9,157 foot summit, over 6,000 feet of elevation gain within 28 miles. Now I know the strengths of the Elite and its two weaknesses. The first I had experienced yesterday, long straight high speed cruising; the second would come today, steady, slow speed climbing in high ambient temperatures. We were surprised and delighted. The Princess gathered up her skirts and simply held steady at about 3,500 rpm in third as we went round corners, on straightaways and occasionally burst to 6,000 to get round a dump or delivery truck. The temperature stayed right at 90 degrees C and oil pressure never varied off 40 psi. We stopped about halfway up at an overlook and to give Gary a stretch, and met a delightful couple from England on holiday that recognized the Elite and many other cars as they passed. They even understood about Gary taking a stretch break and helped him get his bearings.

After a welcome coffee (and bathroom) break at the Mt. Lemmon Café in Summerhaven we had an equally fun run back down to the desert floor and the Pima Air and Space Museum. On the way we passed Davis Monthan Air Base and what the locals call "the Boneyard"; literally thousands of decommissioned military aircraft. Virtually any aircraft from the jet age is represented by the hundreds lined up row after row in quite military precision. Your tax dollars at work!

The Pima Museum was fascinating…so much so that Ann and I decided to forego the afternoon loop of the drive and stay to look at everything we could. From JFK's actual Air Force One, to the X-1 rocket plane, to the X-15 and the B-52 with the wing mount that carried it to the top of the atmosphere. A functioning mission control and space shuttle module reproduction, was history to be touched and at full scale too. Fantastic!

The early afternoon back at Starr Pass meant we could take a nap and still be right on time for drinks and dinner. Another lovely evening in Tucson, which Ann and I decided we liked much better than the concrete and manicured Phoenix.

The drive through the saguaro and sand west of Tucson found us in convoy with the Delahaye most of the morning. It was quite a contrast from the older technology, bigger powered sports car of the thirties to the tiny but advanced thinking of Lotus. We passed each other several times, not so much to get ahead as to find another view to appreciate. At the end of the day, each of us was quite complimentary to the other regarding the beauty, mechanical correctness and pure pleasure of sharing the moments.

The lunch destination was Firebird Raceway in Chandler, home of the Bob Bondurant Racing School. We had a quite excellent meal, especially considering typical racetrack food, and then we got to play. Not only were we allowed to run on the track at fairly aggressive speeds behind a pace car, but also to run an autocross course in the school's Pontiac Solstice convertibles and run a kart track in their karts. The Princess acquitted herself very well keeping up with a Ferrari 250 GT except on the main straight. After about a dozen laps though, I saw oil pressure dropping in left hand turns and decided that discretion should rule the day so I came into the paddock. Shame, too, as I was catching the Ferrari by getting a launch off the last corner onto the straight!

The Elite takes the last turn onto the front straight at Firebird

After the day at Bondurant, we drove back to Phoenix and the Ritz Carlton for a lovely banquet, silent auction and awards presentation. There were many awards for various clever things but the one award that several cars didn't get was the finishing award. Two cars never made it past the first day; one, a '60's American car, was fixed several times and still didn't make it to the finish. The mechanics worked on over thirty different problems involving over twenty cars. One car didn't need a bit of attention though…the Princess. One and a half quarts of oil and less than 29 gallons of gasoline, plus a little polish and clean was all she needed to handle it all: High mountain passes, climbs, twists, long high speed runs on the Interstate, hot city traffic…nothing fazed her.

In August 2007 Peter Egan drove her home from LOG 27 in Aspen, CO over 12,000 foot Independence Pass and into Denver, a distance of about 200 miles. He had never driven an Elite before despite his affection for things Lotus. His observation is perhaps the most perfect I can summon to express my affection for the Princess.

He wrote in the March 2008 issue of Road & Track: *"Lovely car; delicate steering and an elegantly simple envelope of a cockpit, like the inside of a small, private, spaceship. And, like all Lotuses, it was an overachiever, easily going way too fast for a 1.2 liter car. Maybe it really was too fast; these cars had their suspension pickup points anchored in a fiberglass body shell after all and were famously prone to stress cracks. Ross said he'd checked the car over thoroughly and it was fine. Nevertheless, I slowed down just a bit".*

"I know you aren't supposed to write while you drive, but on a long downhill straight near Shawnee, I dug a notebook and pen out of my pocket and scrawled the words 'A fragile ecstasy'. The word 'fragile' here was not so much a description of the Lotus, I think, as of ecstasy itself. It comes to us fleetingly, in only the best cars."

Oh, how Gary, Ann and I agree.

11 A GREAT BUNCH OF LOUTS

What would you think if you saw a vacation trip offer that went something like this?

"One week in England and France for two; includes touring to the Classic Le Mans event. Be met at the Heathrow airport and taken to your private accommodation in a home in the Ashdown Forest. Then, after a sumptuous dinner and a good night's rest, be personally driven to Gatwick airport for a short flight to Manchester where you will be met by a chauffeured Bentley Flying Spur and driven to pick up your new Elise 111R. Follow the thorough directions to Chesterfield to a farm where you will be greeted with a suitable drink, dinner and a private suite. Depart the next morning driving through the wonderful A and B roads to Poole, where you will board a high speed catamaran ferry as seen in a Bond movie with hundreds of other enthusiasts in classic cars and waft your way to Cherbourg. Then convoy along the nearly vacant French roads to a private suite in a restored old stone farmhouse just 35 miles from the LeMans track. Stay with other devoted Lotus fans and celebrate with dinner and drinks each evening, then head off in convoy to the race track in the mornings where you will park in a dedicated Lotus corral inside the Bugatti circuit. All food, lodging, car rental, both ferry crossings and tickets for full access at Le Mans are included. Total cost for the week - $636.00"

If this sounds too good to be true, you don't have the right connections, the right friends, or the right tour planning entity. Luckily, Ann and I do!

We met Geoff Cole, Brian Green and Rod Thonger in 2005 when they came to the USA as part of the Se7ens Tour that year. Out of about 50 Sevens type cars of various origins (Caterham, Westfield, Birkin, Stalker, Robin Hood and some specials and hybrids) there were only three real Lotus Sevens. Geoff's, with Brian as copilot, Rod's and mine. Interestingly they were all Series 3 cars within 50 chassis numbers of each other. Over the weeks of the tour we became good friends, even to the extent of installing the prop shaft from my dead car into Geoff's car so he could make it up the Pacific Coast Highway. At the end of the trip party in San Francisco, Rod suggested a new organization with the three of us as charter members; **LOUTS** – **L**otus **O**wners **U**p **T**o **S**omething!

With a name like that, of course we had to meet expectations, so in 2006 Ann and I went to England for the Goodwood Revival, stayed with Rod and Liz Thonger in Nutley in the Ashdown Forest, and Brian and Liz Green in Lincoln. We had a ball as I detailed in a previous story, "A Pilgrim Goes to Lotus". Then in 2007, they all came over to Colorado for LOG 27 where they stayed at our house and were able to drive several of my Lotuses to Aspen and back. As Peter Egan wrote: *"Picture a fox hunt, with cars instead of horses and hounds"*. The bond got stronger.

So, in 2008, they reciprocated. As Ann and I had wanted to see LeMans for some time, I inquired whether the LOUTS were interested in such a trip. It turns out that Geoff and Brian had already begun planning such a trip with the North Yorkshire Lotus Owners Club, (acronym NYLOC, or as they call themselves, "The plastic nuts").

Now, Geoff has organized tours for years for his friends to Grands Prix around the UK, Europe and even the US, so this was no challenge for him at all. He self-deprecatingly calls his adventures "Rough and Ready Tours". I, of course, interpreted this to mean "things could get rough so you'd better get ready" tours. Not so! Geoff procured the hire car Elise, made the luxury ferry arrangements and booked our flight from Gatwick to Manchester. Meanwhile, Brian was working in concert with the French Lotus Owners Club who had reserved a club block of tickets to the event, had a paddock dedicated to Lotus and even a reception tent with champagne. He also owns a villa in a tiny French town called Souge`, not far from LeMans. All we had to do was redeem hundreds of thousands of miles to get from Denver to London, and pack for fun. Rough indeed!

Upon landing in England, we were in good hands right away. Rod met us at Heathrow and drove us to he and Liz' home for a lovely dinner and a much needed sleep. The next morning we were driven to Gatwick airport not far from their home and had a short flight to Manchester where a proper English chauffer in a cap, unfortunately not named James, met us with a sign and walked us to a waiting Bentley Flying Spur where we wafted our way in coddled comfort (Pass the Grey Poupon!) to an elite car hire company called Lambogenie. Geoff had arranged with the owner, Russ, for us to have either a Lotus Europa or an Elise. I was intrigued with experiencing the Europa, a car we never got in the USA, but we agreed that the Elise with a removable top would be more versatile, albeit smaller - a choice that would have consequences later.

After thorough instruction and documentation we were off to Sheffield to meet Geoff at his friend Dan's home. We had very clear step by step directions which we managed to follow for at least 200 yards before a wrong turn, a problem that would be regularly repeated throughout the day. At one point we found ourselves in the middle of a bus terminal in the center of the city where only busses and ignorant American tourists were found. I'm still not sure how we got out of there but I do remember being prepared to explain to any policeman that stopped us for going the wrong way on a one way street that we *were* only going one way. I resist GPS devices at my peril!

At last we arrived at Dan and Steph's home in Sheffield where the hospitality was as good as if we were old long lost friends though we had just met. I guess Geoff must be a very good friend for us to get treated so well as his friend. The next morning we joined with Dan and Geoff who were in Dan's Morgan and meandered down the "B" roads to Poole on the south coast. Not having to worry about directions (we simply followed Dan) we got to enjoy the beautiful English countryside and charming towns. In Poole we met up with a dozen or so others who were headed for France as well. We stayed at a Travelodge near the port and had a wonderful evening with dinner, drinks and looking over the variety of cars in the car park outside. Rough & Ready Tours had booked us on the high speed hydrofoil ferry I'd only seen in the Bond films before so we prepared for an early morning departure. We went to sleep at a reasonable hour only to be awakened by a fire alarm at about 2:00 am.

After clearing out of the room, down the hall and out into the car park with all the other guests it was determined that the alarm was false and we all went back to attempt sleep. It didn't come, of course, until it was almost time to rise again. Sleepily we got to the cars and into the ferry queue. By now hundreds of cars had gathered and most were classics. It was a visual treat and fascinating to watch those with low clearance creep aboard.

Getting aboard was an adventure in packaging. We were directed to a certain ramp, then to a specific deck and place based on our size. As each car was directed in to its place, we were given just a minute to get our things and depart for the passenger deck. I was a bit slow and so another car was placed about a foot from ours before I got out. Unfortunately an Elise door must be wide open to even clear the sill and allow exit. There was no way I could get out that door. Ann had already been directed to the stairwell so I was all alone in my predicament. After contemplating a channel crossing in the hold of the ferry all alone, I had a spark of an idea. If I rolled the soft top back I could climb out the top! So that's what I did. Not very elegant yet practical - the accommodations above deck were far, far better. If we had selected the hardtop Europa, I would have been there for the whole crossing!

Having never been on a hydrofoil of this size, Ann and I were delighted with the speed and comfort. We had been warned that if seas were high, the ride would be really rough but we were ready (get it?) with our Dramamine though we never needed it. Instead we ran into a couple from England who saw our LOG 27 logos on our jackets and said they had some good friends who put on that event in Colorado. We replied that we had been involved in it as well. It turned out their good friend were our good friends too, John and Carole Arnold. So we all joined together singing *"It's a Small World After All"*.

The trip from Cherbourg to Brian and Liz' home in the little town of Souge` was a delight. Big sweeping roads of perfect asphalt and pretty little towns every so often were the norm as we fairly flew along. We passed and were passed by a wonderful variety of classic cars usually in packs of four to eight...mates on holiday to Classic LeMans.

Our arrival at the house in Souge` was met with ample food and drink and about twenty five of the most enthusiastic Lotus nuts you can imagine. The NYLOC ladies had planned a dinner at a local restaurant so we went to the most wonderful French dinner (if they served a crumpled paper plate with the sauces and garlic they use it would have been fantastic but this was tender beef) and listened to the plans to get to the track the next day. We were going to LeMans!

Once we got to LeMans, the experience was beyond my wildest expectations. Around 450 cars were entered in six groupings, by age, and prepared to perfection. Pick a car that competed in the last 80 years at LeMans and it was probably entered. Blower Bentleys from the late '20's? *Check.* Ferrari TdF and GTO from the early '60's? *Check.* C type and D type Jaguars from the mid '50's? *Check.* Porsche 917 long tail and Ferrari 512 from the '70's? *Check!* And, most iconic of all to me, more than half a dozen Ford GT40's. For us yellow and green fanciers there were numerous Elites and Elan 26Rs registered. They gave good accounts of themselves too. I watched a 26R stay right with a GT40 through the Dunlop curves and the new chicane all the way to Tetre Rouge where the GT 40 disappeared as the power of the Ford became obvious within the first few hundred yards of the Mulsanne straight– which, ironically with two chicanes, isn't a straight anymore because of the modern speeds. Still the circuit is iconic despite all its alterations.

The Dunlop Bridge proved to be a perfect vantage point for watching cars come up the hill that was steeper than I had envisioned from the TV coverage of the 24 hours. Sitting on the bank, drinking a fine beer and eating a jambon et fromage baguette (That sounds so much more elegant then ham and cheese sandwich, doesn't it?) while watching and listening to a phalanx of GT 40's chase each other up the hill was more special than I can describe.

But it wasn't only the cars on the track that captivated me. In the paddock, we were able to get right next to such a wonderful variety of cars – cars that weren't just in a magazine photo any more but in the full richness of steel, fiberglass or aluminum within touching distance. And their owners and drivers were only too willing to discuss their involvement there. For most, it was a longtime dream fulfilled. Even for those who had been to several Classic LeMans events, it was apparent that they were still very appreciative of their good fortune to be able to play on that hallowed track. And in the surrounding car parks, most dedicated to a single marque, I was told that there were over 6,000 classic cars. In the Lotus corral were an estimated 300 Lotuses, certainly more than I had ever seen in one place before. From the Mark 3, registered LMU 5, to the latest Exige S, Sixes, even one with a custom body, Sevens restored to perfection, a dozen Elites, Elans of every series and Plus 2's, with drophead conversions too, and every more modern Lotus – Elise, Exige, Esprit, Europa, Eclat, Excel. It was "E" overload!

The historic LeMans start was especially fun to watch. Each group started its first session with drivers sprinting across the track to the waiting car at the flag drop. Of course, modern safety requirements meant that they had to go around the short Bugatti circuit where belts and safety gear were checked then proceed past the start line on a rolling start, but the image of the old days will always stay with me. Each group was on track three times so that each was able to experience a full daylight session, a sunset or dawn session and a nighttime session. Unlike the real 24 hour race, the Classic participants only tasted the extremes of the demands of the full day, but there was track action for the full 24 hours, almost like the real thing. And there was no rain either – sunny and temps in the mid-seventies. I told you Rough and Ready Tours was good!

Meanwhile, back at the villa, we had a magnificent dinner and a pretty good gathering of Lotuses of our own, such as an Exige with *a removable top!*, a beautifully restored Elan Sprint, a red M100 Elan and a couple of almost but not quite matching yellow Europas. It was a setting that was almost impressionist; especially as the sun didn't set until nearly 10:00 pm. Country France on a summer's eve…I will happily go back if they'll have me.

After LeMans, we expected a somewhat anticlimactic end of the trip as we had to make our way back to England and get a more mundane hire car for the rest of our visit. As has happened on so many Lotus outings, things changed rapidly. But first, the return to the ferry early on the morning of Bastille Day was magical.

We were to meet some of our group, who had been another place, in the town square in front of the church in Fresney at 6:00 am. The drive to the square took us through some open fields where the mist was floating ethereally on the ground, and then through several small villages. As we flew along the narrow, deserted streets in the twilight of dawn, the sound echoing off the stone walls of the buildings directly adjacent to the road, and as the headlights washed over the curves of the statues in the town square, it occurred to me that we were living our own version of C'était un rendezvous by Claude Lelouch. Then, upon our arrival in the square, a small van disgorged six young revelers who had apparently taken it upon themselves to make sure that Bastille Day was not forgotten, as they danced, sang and generally made joyful noise in the center of the sleepy village. At their urging we left with dramatic double black stripes of smoking tires on the asphalt to cheers of approval.

The plan was to return the Elise to Gatwick airport the next morning, but we never made it. Passing through a roundabout near Chichester, just south of Goodwood, a large plume of acrid smelling smoke erupted from the rear hatch of the Elise. I flagged down Rod Thonger in his Seven and we pulled off to the roadside layby. Ann had opened the hatch and Rod was ready with the fire extinguisher while I labored to extricate myself from the diabolically tight driver's side. Ferry déjà vu! With the hatch open we could see there was no immediate danger. We thought perhaps the valve cover gasket was leaking oil on the exhaust header. I had been very carefully instructed to call Dave at Lambogenie any time of day or night if I had trouble, so that is what I did. After describing the situation he wanted to call an expert on the Elise before allowing me to continue. When he called back he conveyed that when the normally reliable Toyota engine in the Elise exhibits an oil leak from the valve box, the engine is at or near terminal meltdown, so I was to wait for the recovery service to pick up the car. While Liz rescued Ann and all the luggage, I waited with Rod in a car park about a mile on until the car was recovered and then rode with him to his home in Nutley in quite spirited fashion in his lusty Seven. I was disappointed that we hadn't finished the trip in the Elise, and concerned that I might be liable for damages as well.

Nonetheless, after another stay with Rod and Liz, and an awe filled visit to the preserved Bodiam Castle that was built in the late 1300's which Liz thoughtfully organized, we continued on with our plans with a trip to Salisbury and a visit with our friend Gordon Morris and his lovely wife Jan. We had a delightful visit with them at their charming home, sitting in the glass conservatory listening to the canaries and playing with the dogs. Gordon then showed us around the "close", the walled part of the city of Salisbury then through the Cathedral and finally a shop where I bought a proper flat cap while Ann got sweaters and a scarf. The next day while the ladies went shopping, Gordon and I went for a drive in his perfect Seven S2 and Elan S4, alternating along the way so that I could contrast the two. The Seven felt quite strong and direct while the Elan was more civilized yet no less capable of rapid transit through the narrow English lanes. A delightful pair of cars cared for by a delightful man.

We spent the last two days of our magical two weeks in the Cotswold's and fell in love with them. There is a town called Bourton-on-the-water which is a must see if you are ever out that way. I have heard people gush about the beauty and serenity of the Cotswolds for years and now, finally, I understand. As lovely as we found all the places we visited, this will hold a special place in our memory. After two days of idyllic rest, we found our way back to the maze that is Heathrow and actually found the rental car return. A long tiring flight home left me basking in the wonderful memories and, alternatively, worrying about the fate of the Elise and my responsibility.

A few days after our return I got an email from Geoff who was following up on the status of the Elise. It said:

> *Ross,*
>
> *I received a call today from Russ at Lambogenie. He said they had carried out a thorough investigation which indicated the engine had been ragged to 10,000 rpm on several occasions!*
>
> *Then he laughed, the @#*&%$@!*
>
> *When they started the engine Russ could smell something burning, so Dave removed the undertray and found a melted plastic wallet that contained info to customers on the procedure to follow if they needed to get the car recovered!*
>
> *I think they call that irony.*

Apparently, while packing a quart into a pint pot, for that is a pretty close approximation of the Elise's boot capacity, I had let the plastic folder that held the paperwork slip over the divider between the boot and engine. In time it had worked its way into contact with the exhaust. That was all there was to the engine meltdown.

All's well that ends well they say and this ended very, very well. It has been said that doing is better than having, and, while I subscribe to that philosophy as regards things, I think that having good friends allows far more doing. And my friends having things like Lotus contacts and cars of their own allows even more doing.

Thank you my fellow LOUTS!

12 THE PRACTICAL LOTUS
...and the Impractical Way I Got It.

After a LOCO outing one summer's day in 1999, (LOCO being the acronym for Lotus Colorado, and, more apt than you'd think at first glance) wherein I had a chance to drive Jim Collins' M100 Elan, I thought I should get one. This Elan is quite different from the original Elan in time (1965,1991) and design (Front wheel drive, transverse turbocharged engine, eight inches longer but a foot wider, it even has air conditioning) I was well and truly hooked. This is a car that does everything well – it's quick, fast, handles well, has lots of room, even trunk space for two, and is a convertible. With sudden summer rainstorms common in Colorado, that is a very nice attribute, since my Seven has no weather protection and the top on my Elan takes a solid ten minutes to erect by which time the rain may well have passed leaving everything including the top erector soaking wet.

But M100 Elans are sort of funny looking in that they are very wide for their length. In a word they look...stubby. To maximize the car's appeal color becomes very important and I therefore decided if I were to get one it would have to be yellow or nothing - Norfolk Mustard yellow to be precise. Now, there were only 546 M100 Elans ever imported to the USA of all colors and of these only 53 were Norfolk Mustard yellow. The movie "Honey, I Shrunk the Kids" used about five, leaving only forty some yellow cars out there, less than one per state. The other thing about M100 Elans is that I was not the only one who was aware of how fun and practical a ride it is, so most owners were holding on to theirs. My search took over a year and went far afield.

I found one in Phoenix and was well into negotiations; the seller and I had agreed on a price. The next day he sold it to someone else for more and told me to go suck eggs. I was back to square one. I had seen a car in Hawaii, but thought it would be too expensive and difficult to get it back to the mainland. Nonetheless, I was pretty much out of options so I inquired about that car. To my surprise, the very nice woman selling the car was in the import business in Honolulu and had close ties with several shipping companies. She was only too willing to give me a fixed price including shipping to any of three US ports – Long Beach or Oakland CA, or Tacoma, WA. Since my daughter lives in Seattle, Tacoma was the easy choice. So I bought the car and waited for shipping dates to be determined so I could plan my flight to Seattle-Tacoma. A few weeks later I flew to SeaTac where my daughter met me to give me a ride to the port of Tacoma and the waiting Elan on the 4th of December 2000. I now had 1,350 miles to get home.~ In a car I had only seen in photos.~ Over the Continental Divide.~ In winter. Well planned, Ross. Well planned!

For those of you not familiar, as I was not, with transporting a car on a ship, there are a few ironclad rules. The first is that the car must be shipped with a minimal amount of gasoline in the tank. The second is that the longshoremen are in control - until they tell you that you can touch the car, you stay away. So it was that I could see the little yellow car which was technically mine but I could not get near it for about 45 minutes while they searched the car and reviewed my paperwork. Think of a TSA body cavity security screening but without the nice uniforms.

At last it was time to get my car! I opened the door and slid in to sit in her for the first time. She looked pretty good - at least as good as the photos so that was a relief. I stuck the key into the ignition switch and turned it. Nothing! Zip, Nada, Zilch. Not even a click. The door light cast a feeble glow so I knew there was some power but not enough to even trigger the solenoid. Well they must have a source to jump a battery I thought. This couldn't be the first time a car had arrived with a dead battery, so I went in search of one of the port guys. When I found one he said he had a jump start cart since this happens all the time. Apparently the continuous small drain of the electronics in more modern cars, such as this modern car from 1991, is enough to deplete the battery in the two weeks or more from drop off in Hawaii to pick up in Tacoma.

So back to the Elan we went with the jump cart. I opened the hood to hook things up and there was no battery. "Oh, it must be in the trunk", I said. I closed the hood with gusto and went to open the trunk where I found: exactly nothing. So here I am in the Port of Tacoma with a willing but impatient longshoreman expecting me to know this car I am seeing for the very first time. I did the only thing I could think of, something very out of character for me. I got out the owner's manual and looked up the location of the battery. It turns out that it is under the soft top stowage compartment behind the cockpit, and it requires three steps to get to it. Unlatch the soft top and lift it forward, away from the back deck of the cockpit, and while holding it just so, release the latch for the deck cover, tilting it rearward. Then with your third hand, while holding the two other parts, lift the cover which forms the bottom of the storage compartment in order to access the battery. Now, with another hand while holding all these, attach the jumper cables to the correct posts in the dark "well" and simultaneously walk around to the driver's seat and twist the key. Easy! Luckily, my longshoreman was a "car guy" and willing to assist and even more luckily, she started right up with the jump. Problem one - Man solved.

Problem two presented itself immediately as the low fuel light shone brightly now that there was juice from the alternator. So, Mr. Longshoreman, "Where is the nearest gas station?" I query. He gives me directions and, with my daughter following, I prayerfully head out of the Port to the byzantine array of streets hoping I can find this mythical gas station while trying to familiarize myself with the controls of this strange car, all before I run out of fuel.

Well, we found the gas station after only one small detour and as I pulled up to the pumps I decided to leave the car running for a couple of reasons. First, I had no jumper cables and had no desire to go through that Rube Goldberg process again and, two, it was only about 37 degrees F and I wanted to get some heat into the car for my trip. I like my comfort! The gas door on the Elan is right behind the driver's door and has a remote release. But where? Again with the manual and I am beginning to feel like a rookie driver. I find it and open the filler door, put the nozzle into the tank with the auto shutoff set and go off to clean the windshield. Scrubbing away I get a vague sense of something wrong as I get a very strong smell of gasoline. I turn away from my windshield cleaning and realize I am standing in a lake of gasoline which is coming from beneath my still running car and the still running pump. Seeing a potential "Towering Inferno" I run over, stop the pump, hang the hose and roll the car away from the spill, trailing gas as I go.

After getting off the asphalt and onto the graveled area, I shut off the car figuring I can bump start it if I have to but I really don't want to deal with a fire. Now I must wait for the leak to stop though it still drips steadily from the gas tank onto the parking lot gravel and disappears. After about 10 minutes the dripping has stopped. During that time I had called Hawaii on my cell phone and reached Cindy the seller. "What the hell is the story with the leaking gas tank," I cry. "Oh yeah, I forgot to tell you" she says, "You can only put in about 7 ½ gallons or it will leak out a crack on the side of the tank. That gets you about 200 miles though so don't worry...just don't overfill it and you'll be fine!" OK, I put that on my list of things to deal with when I get home. For now I can only get 2/3 the range per normal tankful so I will just have more stops. My daughter shakes her head in a gesture that says "This is my ancestral lineage? I'm toast!" She gives me a hug, wishes me well, and gets in her reliable Toyota built sedan with a look that says "Don't call me when that thing breaks down like I know it will" I wave goodbye and start for Colorado, now only 1,345 miles away.

As I head south on Interstate 5 toward Portland where I will turn east along the Columbia River, I fiddle with the heating and lighting controls. Now I know I could have looked these up in the manual too, but where's the fun in that? I get the lights and wipers figured out but no matter what setting I choose for the heating and vent, all I can get is cold air. It isn't bad here in Washington, though I'm not exactly comfortable, and we have already established that I do like my comfort, but when I get into the high altitude parts of Idaho, Utah, Wyoming and Colorado, I want HEAT! Remembering that my old racing buddy Jim Hegy has a brother in Olympia WA which I am just entering, I call him to get brother Bill's number. Calling Bill I get lucky again. He is at home and says come on over. He has tools, knowledge and a garage...the traveler's trifecta!

After a short scenic drive I find Bill's house out on a beautiful point by Puget Sound. After showing me around his perfect setting and lovely home, Bill starts looking at the engine compartment. In only a moment he says, "I see the problem. The heater hoses have been cut and plugged." Apparently, in an effort to get better air conditioning performance, someone took the heater core out of the system to make sure no residual heat got through. In a few minutes we had the hoses reconnected added some coolant to the now larger capacity system and...wait for it... we got warm air from the heater vents! Now fully equipped to take on the Arctic, I thanked Bill and headed for Colorado, now only 1,335 miles away. Are you sensing a pattern here?

Off I went, cruising serenely toward Portland and getting comfortable with the car. It really did drive well and had plenty of spunk. I even got a few honks and thumbs up as I cruised down I-5. One thing did begin to bother me though. The top which was supposed to seal against the cockpit deck, didn't. There was about an inch gap pretty much across the whole back and the amount of cold air that came in was prodigious. At temperatures in the high thirties it was an annoyance but at much colder temperatures I was expecting across the Rockies it would be downright cold. So at my first overnight stop in eastern Oregon, I attempted a duct tape repair to seal the void. The next morning I was pleased as I briskly accelerated to I-84. It lasted all the way to the end of the entrance ramp. Flapping duct tape adds so much ambiance to a road trip doesn't it?

Over the pass from Pendleton to Baker City Oregon I wended my way, heat fully on. This kept my feet and face warm but the cold air on the back of my neck was only solved by a parka with a hood that I pulled up tightly around my head. Down through Idaho, even with stops every 200 miles or so to refuel, I made pretty good progress. The Elan felt very comfortable at a 3,500 rpm cruise which translates to about 75 miles an hour; a rate that made good progress without attracting any law enforcement. This was the fastest speed I had ever made on one of my trips to bring home a Lotus I had found. As the fellow who fell off the top of the Empire State Building said to the window washer as he passed by at the 58th floor…"So far so good".

Just as I was about to enter Utah, the snow began in earnest. Now I understand the name of the first "town" in Utah on I-84. It is called Snowville. Just a gas station, café and seedy motel, the place certainly earned its name that day. It was snowing at a rate of an inch per hour, but was I nervous? No. The defroster, the heater and the wipers all worked and I can explain why. This was the first Lotus I knew of where the electrical stuff was Delco instead of Lucas, one of the few benefits of General Motors ownership stake in the late 1980's and early 1990's. Gradually, the road headed downhill toward Salt Lake City, the weather improved and the snow turned to rain and then diminished altogether. Just past Ogden, I-84 turns east and goes through a lovely valley toward its junction with I-80 east of the Wasatch Range. Stopping for gas again I took off layers of clothes as the weather had improved so much that I actually welcomed the breeze from the gap in back. Refueled and refreshed with a power meal of a Snicker's bar and a Coke, I felt so good I actually thought about driving straight through to Denver even though it would mean a post-midnight arrival. As I mentioned about passing the window washer at the Empire State building earlier, I wasn't done yet.

Almost immediately after turning east on I-80 the snow started again. The temperature dropped as the road gained altitude, and the wind picked up. Within five miles I was in a full-fledged winter storm. I put my parka back on and cranked up the heat. For the first time, I was glad this Lotus had front wheel drive. It was as stable as – well – a stable. I pressed on. The sky got darker and the wind got stronger. I pressed on. Along the side of any interstate highway are these green steel T posts with little round white reflectors on top about 250 feet apart. Normally I barely notice them but today I did. The little reflector would shine back at me out of the frenzied flakes that made me feel like I was in one of those little winter scene snow globes you shake up to make a storm. Finally, the visibility was so bad that I was actually driving from post to post. Each time I would pass one of these posts, my headlights could just pick up the next reflector. So for the next thirty miles or so, over an hour at the speed I was going, that is how I drove -focused on the right side of the road so I wouldn't go off into a ditch or into the oncoming lane it was exhausting since the big rig truckers could apparently see much better from their elevated perch and would come roaring by in a swirl of white.

Slowly but steadily I climbed the grade and made it into Wyoming. At Evanston, just inside the Wyoming line, I pulled off the Interstate to get fuel and recharge the battery. Not the car's–mine! I was wiped out. All my focused energy meant I gripped the wheel so tightly my hands hurt.

My plan to get home that night was shelved. I would be happy to make Rock Springs. Even this plan was soon put paid as I was told by a state trooper who came into the gas station office where I was warming up a bit, that I-80 was closed both directions until further notice. I got back in the Elan and drove into beautiful downtown Evanston - about ¼ mile. There I got the next to last room in a motel, walked across the parking lot to a diner, had some supper, walked back to the motel room and went to sleep. I was toast.

I slept so soundly I had no idea how bad the storm had been when I awoke the next morning. I found a white hump about the size of a VW Bug where my tiny Elan had been the night before. 15" had fallen they said and it was mighty cold. Maybe there would be another night in snow bound Evanston. After brushing the snow away with my gloved hands, (why would I have a snow brush with me?) I tried to start the poor, cold car. To my surprise and delight it fired right up. I cleaned the rest of the car a bit better while the defroster did its job on the windshield and then I decided to attempt a circle around the motel parking lot as a trial run to see if I could even make forward progress through the deep snow. As it turns out the Elan is a pretty good snow car. The FWD and the front air-dam let it just doze a path through the soft snow of the parking lot. I felt like a trailblazer! So, I loaded my stuff and myself into the car and headed for eastbound I-80. Homeward Bound!

Upon reaching the entrance ramp, I found that the big rigs had already created a rut path up the ramp and onto the highway. All the trucks that had preceded me, who had got an early start while I was still dreaming, seemed content to follow in the same path at about 25 mph. This meant that the snow that had been pushed out of the ruts made a hard pack between lanes about 18" tall so changing lanes would be virtually impossible. I did what anyone with a low clearance car would do...I stayed in the conga line of trucks at 25 mph. After about an hour or so the snow depth tapered off, and by the time we passed Little America I was able to change lanes and increase my speed to about 35 mph. At this rate I could do the 380 miles home by midnight. Arrrghh!

The further east we went the lower snowfall levels were and by Rock Springs the snow was pretty minimal. At the same time temperatures were rising and what little snow there was started melting. Now I could change lanes at will! My speed increased along with my spirit and the rest of the trip home was pretty routine at speeds more like I had been achieving in Oregon and Utah before the snow. I pulled into my garage in time for supper, tired but with a sense of achievement at triumphing over a pretty big storm in a pretty small car.

Some changes needed to be made and they were. Lotus Cars USA replaced the gas tank under a warranty recall so I could fill it to the top, (even though it was nearly 10 years old; Thanks LCUSA) and I had a new top installed properly so it sealed as it was supposed to. I got a new set of tires and wiper blade assemblies, had a stereo installed and gave her a good clean and polish. She has been our faithful companion ever since, carrying Ann and me to lots of places in Colorado, New Mexico and Wyoming, but never again in a snow storm. If we ever did get into one though, I'll bet we'd do fine...this is a practical Lotus!

The Modern Elan - The M100; Stubby but fun and practical.

13 LOG MATH

**Four Guys plus Two Cars equals One Great Adventure
to the 30th Lotus Owners Gathering in Gettysburg, PA**

After the Saturday Banquet at LOG 30 award for Liars Essay, my fine English friend Rod Thonger observed, "If I had known about this 'Liar's Essay' contest I would have submitted this story:

"On a whim, four guys, two of them quite large and all of them old, decide to drive two small Lotus cars, a 1968 Lotus Seven and a 1965 Lotus Elan, packed with all the gear four guys need to support 8 days on the road and 4 days at a LOG, across highway US 50 to the Atlantic Ocean and on to Gettysburg. They will have a schedule that requires them to make eight lodging waypoints and will make every one exactly as planned.
They will not experience any tribulation through rain, wind or record heat in Kansas and record cold in Cincinnati. They will do 2,345 trouble free miles to LOG as if they were driving new Toyotas.
"Now there is a winning Liar's Essay!"

There is only problem: It's not a lie! That is exactly what we did. Well maybe not exactly, but we made it substantially intact and without any problem that either stopped or materially delayed us. After some careful pre-trip work on the cars by my Yorkshire friends Geoff and Brian, (whose garage is somewhat cheekily referred to as the Lincoln Lotus Centre, [LLC]) our first day began with a great drive down Highway 105 to Monument and breakfast at Village Inn. Only one hour on the road and we had already stopped to eat. Then we stopped again near Rocky Ford, world famous for melons, at Mary's Melons produce stand. As advertised, hers were the biggest and juiciest melons around.

Bent's Old Fort was a revelation to the Brits. The real Old West was brought to life rather than the Hollywood version exported to the world. We got a personalized tour of about two hours covering everything from food to supplies to trades and tourists. We got in free thanks to the old geezer (that would be me) and his Golden Eagle Pass. Driving through eastern CO was extremely hot. We learned later that a new record temp for the date had been set in Garden City ~ 96 degrees.

As we approached Garden City, I remarked that if I had been charged with naming this town, and had at my disposal a full dictionary, the word Garden would never have occurred to me. Farmers were burning their corn and wheat stubble resulting in a smoky haze over the entire town. Until I learned the source I was worried that it was our two Lotus cars that were responsible. Actually, the cars used only a small bit of oil; the Elan averaged about 30 mpg and the Seven about 32. Both ran perfectly.

The next day we got an early start with plans to stop in Dodge City for breakfast. Driving into the rising sun was a challenge and it was quite brisk but by the time we got to Dodge it was perfect. The Brits wanted to see Boot Hill, a tourist trap re-creation of the old front street of Dodge City, but a pretty well done version. We spent two and a half hours there which meant that with our breakfast we had consumed three and a half hours in Dodge. Another slow start. Do you see a pattern forming here?

As we left the city I noticed an auto dealer purveying Chrysler products including Dodge and wondered out loud: "If his ethics were questionable, would he be a Dodgy, Dodge, Dodge dealer?" Driving through Kansas provided a phenomenon I had not ever before seen; the ability to catch a few winks of sleep while driving. No, not me. Brian was at the wheel of the Elan as we proceeded east across miles and miles of dead straight road. His relaxed posture and fixed gaze as we rolled on and on led me to believe it was not only me napping. I looked on the map and warned him of a pair of turns coming up in five miles or so, feeling the whole time that I had stolen precious moments of sleep from him.

At last the turns came, a 45 degree left followed by a 45 degree right only a couple of miles later. Finally, exciting Lotus type of roads in Kansas. But there was more: We encountered a grade which lifted us to a height from which we could see for miles in any direction as though we had reached the summit of a major mountain. Not being familiar with the names of Kansas topography, I enquired at our next stop what it was called. I was informed it is called, in Kansas, an overpass.

Because we had spent so much time in Dodge, we passed up the Kansas Cosmosphere and Space Center and proceeded via a stop in the lovely little town of Cottonwood Falls, to the Tallgrass Prairie where we arrived just as the place closed for the day.

The Tallgrass Prairie from 150 years ago still exists near Council Grove, KS

Well, the visitor center might not be open, but the tall grass has no hours so we took the 1.5 mile walking trail and experienced the immensity of the prairie of a century ago. The wind and the waving grass, the hills and the shifting light that interplayed gave me a sense of what the settlers experienced. The grass was so tall Geoff couldn't be seen in the photo. Then we remembered he was taking the pictures. We got to our hotel in Council Grove, KS and after bathing the prairie off, went to dinner at the historic Hays House, a major supplier and rest stop for those headed west on the Oregon or Santa Fe trail in the early 1800's. We had a great meal and then a detailed personal tour by Dan the manager of all three levels of the famed old place. Lots of human drama within these walls. Neat.

Upon rising and getting ready to leave Friday morning, Geoff told us that Brian had been sick all night and needed medical attention. Fortunately there is a hospital in Council Grove and after a normal EKG and blood test they determined that he was suffering from acid reflux and not heart problems. Feeling a bit better but still rocky, Brian manned up and we headed east after picking up Rod's laundry from Sylvia at the town Laundromat. She had done it when we were getting Brian treatment. I believe despite multi-tasking, Rod found that Sylvia cost him one sock.

On the road again, as Willie Nelson would say. With a multi hour delay, we drove with intent the rest of the day and bypassed the Mighty Melt Sandwich & Spud Shop a planned must see in Sedalia, MO. Darn! Instead we ate the junk food that we picked up at fuel stops while in the cars, and focused on our target destination of Gray Summit, MO.

When we asked for a dinner recommendation, we not only got a great restaurant but a perfect Lotus road to it. It was six miles of twisty, dipsy-doodle, and blind crests through the woods at dusk. Our euphoria was in direct proportion to the boredom experienced in the flat expanse of

Kansas and Missouri of the past two days because we also had found a great meal.

On Saturday, we awoke to a light rain. That is no problem in the ostensibly weather tight Elan, but presents some difficulty with the Seven having no top or functioning wiper motor. Our fearless LLC lads Brian and Geoff didn't hesitate to jump in and go on the Interstate to downtown St. Louis and the Gateway Arch. I had booked tickets months before so we were able to proceed right to the fascinating elevators that ratchet up the changing angle of the arch as it rises. Quite a view from the top which we enjoyed for about 20 minutes then began looking for one another to go down. Rod, Brian and I found each other readily but there was no Geoff. Now the observation deck of the Arch is only about 50 feet by 12 feet so the only conclusion was that he had gone down already. So that's what we did. Looking for him around the base of the Arch was harder as there is a great museum with lots of displays and other hiding places. We stationed one person at the central information desk and sent scouts to various parts of the monument to find him. Nothing. Finally, I went up the ramp to the glass doors where I could get cell phone reception and found a voice mail from Geoff that he was already with the cars in the parking garage. After reuniting there, I asked why he had gone down ahead of us. He replied, "I couldn't find any of you guys. I thought you'd gone on down" Huh? It's 50 feet by 12 feet!

Getting out of St. Louis on the tangle of intersecting Interstates was tough and we took the wrong exit headed toward Chicago. After a GPS correction and a Wal-Mart stop for gloves, rain gear and a warm hat for Rod (it was getting pretty cold and damp) we took a nice twisty back road to find US 50 east of O'Fallon, IL. The weather cleared a bit although it didn't warm up much, and we made good time across Illinois and through Indiana. The sad thing was Brian and Geoff were still in the Seven so they missed my stirring rendition of "Back Home Again in Indiana" as we crossed the Wabash River. Lucky Rod got to hear it.

I hadn't made reservations for a motel in Bedford, Indiana, our planned stopping point, as there were lots of them and I still had that nagging doubt that we would make a targeted stop that far along the route. Silly me. The cars were running flawlessly. So we found that there were only a few rooms left in the town due to an Indiana University homecoming football game in Bloomington fifty miles away and the overflow crowds who had taken almost all the rooms in Bedford. Our last resort, certainly no pun there, was the Super 8 at $125 per room. Plus tax. Upon departing the next morning I inquired as to the rate the next night; $65 was the answer. This is an illustration of the law of supply and demand!

Onward to our next stopping point – a rendezvous with Eric for lunch just east of Cincinnati at The Dilly Deli in Mariemont, a charming little town resembling an English village. Both the cars and my friends felt right at home. After a delightful lunch and a swapping of Lotus stories we were on our way east again in a record low maximum temp for the date, 46 deg. to Marietta, OH just across the river from West Virginia.

What should have been an easy piece of navigation around Athens, OH became a disaster. Due to multiple construction projects and detours, we ended up circling through the town center of Athens with its abundant stop lights and traffic, and headed the wrong way to reconnect to US 50. We found ourselves way south of where we intended to be and had to find a way back on track. That is where we got lucky; we found Ohio route 681. Trying to find the superlatives to describe it, I can only say "Wow!" A supremely smooth road, devoid of traffic, it dipped and swayed over the Hocking Hills with blind crests and sweeping curves punctuated by an occasional hairpin turn. With Brian leading the way in the Seven driving swiftly, yet within the limit of responsibility, I had as much fun in a Lotus as my very best memories from Colorado's famous mountain roads. It was clearly the best road of the trip we all agreed, even including West Virginia's best. What made it really special, along with the spectacular fall foliage colors, was that, after a disappointment of navigation, it made the high just a bit higher so we arrived in Marietta full of good cheer anticipating tomorrow's roads through West Virginia.

Day six dawned with a light rain and gloomy overcast. We packed up under the hotel portico to stay dry and by the time we were ready to depart, the rain had ceased. Heading over the Ohio River on the old St. Mary's bridge we got stuck behind a very slow truck grinding up the steep grade - so much for fun on the twisting roads. After a long stretch of double yellow lines (it seemed like 20 miles but was really probably half that) we finally got a chance to pass and began driving in a Lotus manner. Onward through the hills on a divided US 50, we were making good time when the rain began again. We ducked off the big slab into the town of Salem for coffee, shelter and Rain-X. We found all three plus fuel at a very friendly convenience store. The magic properties of the Rain-X were revealed to us when, after a thorough application, we found the visibility through windscreen of the Seven to be much improved. It improved mostly because it never rained again all the way to Gettysburg!

Our rate of progress was slow but the grin factor was high as we repeatedly proceeded up and down 9% grades on our way to lunch at the Hilltop Café just east of Romney. We stopped there because it not only looked like a good local eatery, but it had a NAPA parts store next door. After a warm and filling soup/sandwich combo, we were planning to fill the gearbox oil on the Elan. After asking at three places to use a lift and being turned down, we resorted to the old reliable method of one set of wheels on the curb and a bit of help from the jack. Our capable pit and gutter man, Geoff, crawled under the car while Brian and I poured the quart bottle of 90 weight gear oil into a clear tube much like an automotive IV drip. Our safety man Rod, meanwhile, was reaching a very skeptical risk assessment of the whole process.

After more than a quart addition to a 2 pint capacity gearbox (yes you read right) we charged off to our target of Arlington, VA for the night. Passing some beautiful horses and their ranches, we arrived at suburbia just at rush hour. After hitting a dozen or so red lights in a row, we pulled off to have a pint or two (beer not gear oil) and let things clear. The only trouble was when we were ready to do the final bit, the night was completely dark and we were lit. We made it to the hotel just fine only to be joined by several busloads of teen agers on a visit to the nation's capital. Fortunately we checked in just ahead of them but come morning we ran a gauntlet of texting, oblivious teens to our Lotus escape pods.

We sped pleasantly along a parkway that lulled us into a false sense of coping with the maelstrom that is Washington traffic. Soon we were dead stopped for a road repair that funneled three lanes into one controlled by a short green/long red signal and we sat more than we crept. Of course the puny original equipment fan on the Seven failed to cool adequately despite the 60 degree ambient so we were forced to pull off to the side and wait for it to cool. What should have taken minutes took us an hour so when we finally got going, we only stopped briefly along the National Mall alongside which US 50 runs as Constitution Avenue.

Feeling very conspicuous because folks shouted and gawked at every intersection, we were especially taken by an invitation from a couple of DC "professional" women in a Cadillac, with hair color never found in nature, who cooed "Thas' the cutest lil' car I ever did see! You wan' show it to me?" Uh…No. Onward we went after waving to the President as we passed the White House (Geoff is certain he saw a return wave) to meet with Dan Collins in Annapolis for lunch.

One of the cool things about the plans for this trip was the response from people we asked to meet up with us along the way. We had a delightful lunch near the waterfront in Eastport, a bay-front district of Annapolis, at the Boatyard Bar and Grill. Fabulous crab cakes! Both the cars were still running flawlessly and the weather was great. It looked as though we would make our goal of seeing the Atlantic Ocean by sundown a reality.

The eastern shore of Maryland is intricately meandering at the water's edge, but US 50 goes more or less straight through the flat, featureless fields between the bay and the ocean. Thus our progress was quick and it wasn't long before we were closing in on our goal. I held five fingers up in the air for the five remaining miles as a signal to the lads behind. Then four, three, two and one as we approached the beach at Ocean City. As we pulled into the parking lot with the big, arching sign over the board walk, I felt proud we had made it. I gave Rod a high five in the Elan, turned to the Seven, whooped and said that the spirit of Colin Chapman must have been with us. This was proved true when I opened the door to get out and the door fell off. Of Course. True to Colin's mantra of making the thing only strong enough to do the job and no more, we had, after all, *crossed* the finish line.

The Elan and Seven at the Ocean City pier. Ross, Brian, Geoff and Rod
Naturally we spent several hours walking the boardwalk along the beach marveling at the tackiness that is Ocean City, and having a beer and snack at one of the few places not boarded up, as the season was clearly over. That night we repaired the door hinge, the mirror and tended to the transmission and engine oil in a lighted, covered parking area at the

hotel. The opposite side of the supply and demand of Bedford was evident here with thousands of empty rooms. We enjoyed the best hotel bargain of the trip plus a fine bargain meal at Finnegan's the attached Irish pub.

I mentioned that we had crossed the finish line. Not quite. While in one sense we had, after all we had put our focus on making it to the ocean, we still had to get to Gettysburg. This was a portion of the trip on which I had not spent much time planning other than getting us over the top of the Chesapeake Bay via Route One. Leaving it to the GPS system Rod was using, we weaved a quite tangled web of roads around the University of Delaware in Newark, doubling back several times.

Once clear of Newark, we crossed into what we thought was Pennsylvania but must have been England because we encountered the towns of Nottingham and Oxford and roads like Little Britain and Kings Pen. Just as we stopped for a bit of lunch at Pasquale's Pizza we saw the first Amish horse and buggy of the trip. We found the juxtaposition of old English names and Amish carriages and Italian pizza quite humorous. The lads thought it quintessential Americana. Cameras clicked and fingers were pointed. It was like a time warp back to Jolly Old England indeed!

A few hours later we were in Gettysburg and the Eisenhower Hotel alone and the only Lotus cars around but for a lone Esprit. The hotel complex was like a ghost town as we were a day early as we decided to take a day and work on the cars after arrival but before the hordes arrived. As the only inhabitants of the bar, we toasted each other for the successful arrival and the relatively painless trip that none of us secretly believed would be trouble-free, though this was never spoken aloud by any of us.

Actually, contrary to complaint about trouble, the talk in the bar was of doing another long trip. There was even talk about returning to Denver with me and rescheduling the flight to England as the trip had been so smooth and Toyota like. No lie!

14 GOING HOME

Getting to the 30th Lotus Owners Gathering was only half the battle, as detailed in the chapter *LOG MATH*. Here we were in lovely Gettysburg with two cars over forty years old that had already travelled 2,345 miles <u>with</u> the assistance of our riding mechanics from the Lincoln Lotus Centre (LLC) now facing another 1,800 miles without them - only my wife Ann and me in one car each. Now some of you may know that Ann is a great sport about my playing with these old Lotus cars and she accompanies me on most all the trips I take. As a passenger. She had a total of ¼ mile of seat time driving the Seven and had never driven the Elan. So, we put her in the Elan. What, me worry?

Before we could leave, I had a problem to resolve on the Elan. We had attempted to refill the transmission with gear oil after arrival at the Eisenhower only to find the fill plug not removable. It was so stuck that three different attempts with multiple tools and muscles hadn't accomplished anything except making round the formerly hexagon shaped drain plug. If we were to get home it would need to be removable so oil could be added. In fact it needed some to start the trip. During the LOG we had made some halfhearted attempts to find a repair shop without success. Now it was critical. Geoff Cole, while at the NAPA store, had the store suggest "Rooster's Repair". Now, there is a name to inspire confidence, no? Out we went in the country west of Gettysburg to find Rooster. When we finally found the shop, Rooster wasn't there but "Junior" was. He caught me out with his opening line; "I'm only here because I don't work today".

After clearing up that he was not at his "regular" heavy equipment mechanic job, he listened to our tale of woe and said "I have a tool that can loosen any bolt!" After 10 minutes with the super tool, he admitted defeat and suggested high heat. Fearful of Elan flambé, I asked if there were any other way, so he brought out his last resort tool. It was a tapered socket-like affair with teeth that gripped harder when turned anti clockwise. Usually it would be hammered on the offending bolt head but there was no room to swing a hammer here. Instead, using a pry bar for leverage, he applied all the force he could muster on the top of the device and the plug turned. Once removed, he found a suitable plug for the hole, filled it with hypoid oil and we were on our way.

Brian Green, ace LLC guru, had kindly washed both cars and they looked resplendent despite the hard miles already run. Perhaps we should have done that before the Concours the previous Saturday as they really did clean up well, but we had wanted to present them as they arrived with all the patina they had earned. While many spent hours cleaning their cars for presentation, we had, after all, spent eight full days detailing ours. Apparently, the significance of our saga was lost and all they saw was the dirt.

Geoff Cole, the other ace LLC guru, told Ann how to start the Elan as I was already ensconced in the Seven, a procedure that takes many minutes to accomplish, and, also, everyone knows one should never tell a spouse how to do anything. Preparing to leave the Eisenhower Hotel, Ann had only one request. Before we left she wanted to stop to get Heinz Genuine Dill pickles which are not available in Colorado stores. I failed her...we left with no pickles! We made it all the way to Maryland without incident or pickles, a distance of some 15 miles. With only 1,785 more to go, we were practically home.

We had a pretty good experience with West Virginia once Ann began to believe in the powers of the Elan. At the beginning she would follow the recommended speeds for the 9% grades (one over 5 miles long) and twisty curves. These speeds are meant for logging trucks not Lotuses. As Ann put it "When we stopped you told me the Elan could handle these curves better than the Seven. It was those words that inspired me to trust Green Jean". Green Jean, named after my mom, is Ann's pet name for the Elan. As you might imagine our progress picked up dramatically. The hardest part was driving into the setting sun. Some hill angles meant it was directly aimed at us and the low bonnet created a double dose of glare. We made it to Parkersburg, WV in the dark, tired but safe.

Crossing Ohio was uneventful so we were optimistic about our target of Indianapolis for the night until we got on the freeway surrounding the south side. Multiple lanes of big trucks, slow drivers and desperate moves to ramps and exit lanes were a lot to handle, but, again, it was heading into the setting sun that meant trouble. We couldn't read the backlit signs. Just as we were about where I expected our exit to be coming up, I passed under the sign for it. Only then could I read it was closed for repair. Not having a plan "B" I was trying to dead reckon a route when a lady in a minivan slowed dramatically from about 50 mph to about 20 mph to let an 18 wheeler merge in from the right, though he had a long blend lane ahead. I slammed on my brakes and slowed just enough to miss her, hearing a simultaneous screech of tires behind me.

That would be Ann. Luckily, she got stopped and even more luckily, no one was right on her bumper or we would have had a double meat Lotus sandwich. As we shakily passed the lady in the minivan, I noticed her obliviously yakking away on a cell phone. Figures! Finding a side road, we escaped the freeway, stopped and Ann said "That's it! We're off the Interstate until Denver!"

Knowing I had to fill the transmission gear oil every 6-700 miles I planned to do so in Indianapolis in the morning before setting out. The thing was, would it be Ann or me in the gutter crawling under the Elan. Then I had an inspiration…Jiffy Lube. They have all the pieces to do the job and neither Ann nor I would need to get dirty. I found one nearby and we drove over there fully intending to depart toward the west from there. The Elan was handled in quick time after coaxing it over the pit opening that was within a half inch as wide as it's track. The owner even said no charge for topping up, (Still, I gave him $20 since I'm not a regular).

Alas, when turning into the shop, I had hit a curb stop with the sump on the Seven and it had a significant engine oil leak. I said I could keep it filled but the lube shop guy said that would be every 25 miles at this rate of leaking. I sat and thought.

Once again I would find myself at the mercy of strangers, but with an advantage of the big Lotus Ltd. club directory. Picking a name at random from the Indianapolis area in the directory Ann had brought, (one who had noted that he would help travelers) I dialed and got Ben Tackitt. Catching Ben off-guard with my request for a shop that could diagnose and help, he asked to call me back. In about five minutes he called and told me of a shop called Gasoline Alley Tune Up about two miles from where we were. He volunteered to come and lead us there, but I assured him we could find it and meet him there. Good to his word, he was at the shop, right next to the Sarah Fisher Racing Indy Car shop, and the guys were willing and able to take on the repair. Diagnosing a bulging front crank seal, they soon determined all that was needed was a new seal and we could be on our way after a quick installation by Lyle the mechanic.

There was one problem: no seal could be found. Anywhere! Checking all the usual suspects, plus Auto Zone and Checker, as well as the seal distributor who carries every conceivable seal for industry, John found nothing. Nada! Meanwhile I was calling the Lotus suppliers RD and JAE. Both had the seal and could ship it overnight. Not just yet, I said. Not wanting to spend another night in Indy, (nothing personal all you Hoosiers) I asked if they might remember anyone in Indy who had the seal then I could have one shipped to them to replace it. Nope.

Then I had a bright idea that there might be a small engine shop that dealt with Formula Ford prep. It is the same Kent engine. John from Gasoline Alley Tune Up remembered a shop like that about a block away at the other end of Gasoline Alley. When we got there he warned me to not expect much as most of these small shops know what they have but not where they put it and need to scrounge for things. Sure enough, the proprietor, a Kiwi who was just sitting down to eat his sack lunch, allowed as he may have one and would search for it after lunch. "Come back about 1:30" he said. We first turned to go, then I turned and pleaded with him to look now and eat later. Folding down an attic access ladder from the ceiling, he grudgingly climbed into his spares storehouse. Within seconds he reappeared with a New Old Stock Ford part of far better quality than the one that had been on the car. Pulling out my wallet with a $10 bill showing, I asked how much for the seal normally about $5. Looking straight at my hands he said $10. I peeled it off and handed it over. I would have gladly paid $20, even $50, to get back on the road

Back at the shop Lyle kindly deferred his lunch until after the seal was installed and by 12:45 we were on our way. Within a few miles it began to rain so I pulled into a bay of a car wash to get out of the rain (Irony again!) while I got my rain suit on since the Seven has no top. I then got fully over heated while searching for the bottle of Rain-X that I knew was packed there but never could find. The rain would come over the top of the windshield and spit at my face, and both sides of the windshield were obscured For the next hour I think I barely saw the road..

Ann says we drove through some of the prettiest wood lands of the trip with wonderful fall colors made drab and soggy with a heavy rain. One place, the bridge over Walnut Creek, I would love to see again in bright sunlight.

Finally, the rain eased and we stopped for lunch at the Tastee Freeze in Montezuma, IN where we had the best burgers we've had in years. The clouds had cleared so all we had to contend with was a nasty cold north wind as we crossed the Wabash River and made our way to Illinois. We stopped for gas in Springfield and a somewhat knowledgeable local asked "Did you build your Cat-er-Ham?" a Lotus Seven replica built in Caterham England. Pronouncing it correctly, I said "Nope. It's not a Kate-er-um. It's a real Lotus." Not missing a beat he said, "So, who makes Lotus?" A little knowledge is a dangerous thing!

Having gotten a late start, we stopped for the night in Jacksonville, IL. Ann wanted to keep going to Hannibal, MO, but I was beat and it was getting dark fast. The next morning we got up early and drove in quite cold temperatures for a while on our way toward lunch at St. Joseph, MO. Ann had expressed a desire for a burrito of all things so when I spied a Taco Bell logo on an exit sign, we made our exit. Slowing at the Taco Bell, I heard a scraping sound from the Seven but decided to eat first and let things cool down. After lunch it seemed quieter so we made our way to the quick lube for our planned top up of the Elan's transmission oil. By the time we went a half mile the scraping noise in the Seven was a grinding noise. I found the generator fan scraping on the body of the generator. It was clear that the belt had been over tightened; it didn't deflect at all when pushed between the pulleys. I loosened it but to no avail. The bushings were shot and it would not charge the battery. There was but one solution, I pulled out the back up belt I got in tiny Eureka Nevada when I last had this problem and bypassed the generator. Next stop: the local Kmart for a cheap battery charger. Westward Ho!

We continued without problem on US 36 into middle Kansas, to a little town called Belleville, and the S&H Motel, a typical 10 unit motor court from the '50's. After registering I asked if there were an outlet where I might plug in my car for the night. As it turned out there was a regular customer who stayed there a couple of nights a week already plugged into the only outlet. He took core samples from telephone poles in the area, and had two battery chargers to recharge his drill batteries each night for the next day's work. Sharon McGee, the lady that owned and ran the little motel, kindly found an extension cord and a place to plug in so all the batteries could get a full boost. Upon Sharon's high level and strong recommendation we went to dinner at the Belle Villa restaurant in the Elan leaving the Seven to charge.

It turned out to be a great suggestion as Doug, the proprietor, had Tri Tip on the menu. Typically found in central California, (I always have some from the food vendors at Laguna Seca when there) Tri Tip is a particular piece from the bottom of the sirloin prepared with a rub of garlic and salt/pepper that is delicious. I asked Doug how he happened to have this fine delicacy on the menu in the middle of Kansas. He replied "I was taught how to make it by a California buddy while I was in the service. It's always been on the menu in my restaurants". It was excellent! If you are ever in Belleview KS, stop at the Belle Villa. I ate all of mine but Ann couldn't finish hers so we got a little box and took it back to the S&H Motel refrigerator. Before retiring I went to check the battery which was fully charged so I unplugged and went to bed. We, and the battery, were full.

In the morning we awoke to a temperature around 40 degrees so we bundled up and put the Tri Tip in the footwell of the Seven which was just like having it in the refrigerator. After about an hour the car temp and the ambient had climbed and that footwell just behind the exhaust manifold was no longer cold; it was like a warming oven. The Tri Tip was being reheated nicely. When we stopped the meat was a perfect eating temperature, tender and not a bit overcooked. Ahhh, road food!

Gas in western Kansas and eastern Colorado is scarce. I mention this because I did not realize that none of the small towns on the map would have gas stations None. They had post offices, parks, schools, stores, houses and bars, but no fuel. We began to get nervous and I wished I had filled in Bird City, KS. We had stopped at Big Ed's there for lunch upon Dan Crow's recommendation that it was the best steak he had ever eaten and a "Do not miss". The sign said "Ladies Welcome" but apparently they were not, as it was closed. Fortunately the Coors truck was making a delivery and the Coors delivery guy was nice enough to tell us, as he pointed next door, that "right there!" were hot meals. So we each ate an enchilada at the grocery store, "right there".

Once we left Kansas it was at least 150 miles to the first station I knew. When one is low on gas in a small car in big sky country with a "whole lotta nothin" around it tends to lead to worrying. Thankfully we made it to Anton, CO to find a two pump place where nothing had been touched or changed for fifty years. The pumps had to be manually reset, with a spinning glass showing the fuel was being pumped, and there was a uniformed attendant. Looking at his nametag, I read it twice to be sure I saw what I thought I saw…the name Festus. For a minute, as I looked for Matt Dillon and Miss Kitty, Ann thought I'd made a wrong turn and we were back in Dodge City.

We soldiered on into Denver metro rush hour traffic, a real concern for Ann after her Indianapolis stress. We found it was just early enough that we were able to be ahead of the normal rush hour traffic and, using east Colfax instead of I-70, run smoothly to our driveway and switch off with a great sense of accomplishment accompanied by abject relief that we were home safely. The cars had brought us home after 4,141 miles of every kind of road and a wide variety of weather. No disasters and no speeding or other traffic ticket. We had some inconveniences, yet each of these contributed to the adventure rather than ruining it. But we were beat! Ann and I would clean the cars and unpack the junk the next day when I would find the Rain-X *exactly* where I put it in the back of the Seven. Today we would rest and relax from the vibe of the road.

After a few days of recovery and rumination I had the following thoughts regarding:

Scale - The USA is a ***BIG*** place and these Lotus cars we drive are small and vulnerable. It is almost as if the Elan and Seven are ¾ size models of "real" cars and, although they did everything we asked of them, Ann and I felt at risk everywhere there was multi-lane traffic, especially where the big trucks roamed. Clearly, we would have been little more than a speed bump to them. We enjoyed the travel more on the secondary roads, really no surprise, as those are like the English roads for which these cars were designed. Also, there was little or no respect shown to our two tiny green cars that were obviously travelling together. People would pull in between us anytime there was more than a car length gap, making us lose visual contact with each other with a big car in between. It was as if they couldn't even see us. Or, worse yet, they could see us and did it anyway. Sharon at the S&H Motel perhaps said it best with her comment "Those look like keychain cars"

Anachronism –There is a lot missing from cars 42 and 45 years old that we take for granted in a modern car; simple weather protection for example. Even in the Elan with top installed and windows up a surprising amount of rain came in around the joints. Modern cars run at half the RPM for a given speed in top gear so they are much more relaxed. I noted that the Elan turned almost fourteen and a half MILLION engine revolutions on this trip – that's a lot of spinning. Generator, clutch, overheating car (*and* driver) are simply not part of automobile worries in even the most basic modern car. We found 350-400 miles a day was all we could do and we were worn out. We routinely do double those mileages per day in our current cars and are not really fatigued.

Weather & Wind –These are not really a concern for modern cars, while they are key to any trip in an old Lotus. The wind is omnipresent and affects decisions including what to wear and whether to pass. A cool sunny day is a delight but too warm or too cold means discomfort especially sitting in traffic when it is too hot. Rain creates another set of issues and wind and rain together means misery rather than inconvenience. A small temperature change can be felt immediately when going through a valley or over a river. Smells that never reach our noses in a modern car are omnipresent.

All in all, it is an awakening to travel as we did many years ago, both because it shows how far we have come in design and build quality of our cars and because it shows how insulated from the real world we have become in a modern automobile. I shared this with my friend Mike Ingelido upon my return as I was picking up a suitcase he had brought back from Gettysburg for us in his very modern and capable car. He listened to my tales of discomfort and said that I was not the only one who had had difficulty. He stated: "There were two or three times, maybe more, where, for a moment, I completely lost the signal on the XM satellite surround sound".

A Simulation - Several people have asked me what it was like to drive the Seven all that way. Here is the best I can offer.

In your modern car, take two thin pieces of plywood and place them on the seat bottom and back respectively before you sit. Roll down just the two front windows to provide some of the proper buffeting. Turn on the heater to full hot with all the air aimed at the footwell to simulate the engine heat coming off the Seven. Install a heat lamp aimed at the left side of your face. Turn it on. Now, take one bungee cord and wrap it around your legs just above the knees and add another one around your arms and shoulders just above the elbows. If you have a car with selectable gears, find a gear that gives you about 16 miles per hour per 1,000 rpm and accelerate to 4,200 rpm probably second or third gear. Drive 1,800 miles

Of course, that really doesn't complete the experience of being dwarfed by 18 wheelers whose wheel centers are at eye level and where I can read road signs *under* the trailer. Or seeing the sweep of sky and scenery from an open car. Or getting the mesmerizing reflections off the tapered headlight buckets. Or the immediacy of the control input where, as soon as you think it, it happens. Right now. And it certainly doesn't convey the satisfaction of having beaten Kansas in such a car. Or the worry of whether Ann is doing OK in the Elan behind me. Of course she did fine. I wonder how many other wives would be willing to do what she did. What a treasure I have in Ann.

Would we do it again? Probably not such a big trip and probably not on such big roads. Ann said she was glad to be home and had checked that item off her adventure list. Perhaps bungee jumping or steer wrestling for her. Me, maybe I'll take a jaunt down the Mississippi river road from Canada to the Gulf of Mexico with lots of time and an ace Lincoln Lotus Centre riding mechanic along.

Yeah, that's the ticket.

15 WESTFIELD HO!

Nobody needs a Westfield Eleven, a faithful replica of the Lotus Eleven. But if you are like me, a fan of the days of British motorsport when the little cottage industries of Elva, Lola, Mallock and especially Lotus were the forefront of racing car development in the mid 1950's, it would be fun to have an example of the era.

Then reality enters the picture. A Lola Mark 1 or a Lotus Eleven can cost over $100,000. Even for a really well to do fan that is a lot of money, and for one like me with more dreams than dollars, it is out of the question. Fortunately there is an alternative in the case of the Eleven. It seems a fellow in England named Chris Smith restoring a customer Eleven at his shop called Westfield Cars thought that the frame could be reproduced easily, body molds taken from the customer car and with mechanical bits from the Austin Healey Sprite/MG Midget (cars that were, and are, plentiful) a recreation could be easily produced at an affordable price. It was - approximately 180 were made in the mid 1980's.

One of the first in the USA to be captivated by the concept was Peter Egan of Road & Track magazine. After the first article written by Doug Nye announcing the car appeared in R & T, Peter talked the management into a build/drive story on the car. He then wrote a couple of wonderful articles about it, one on the build process called "Crate Expectations" and the other about his and his wife Barb's trip from California to Wisconsin in the newly built and untested car. Titled "Northeast by Westfield" the article likely sold more kits than any advertising Westfield could have done at any price. It certainly sold me!

Not having the mechanical skill or patience of Mr. Egan, yet still having the itch 15 years later, I began looking for a good one already built. Finally, I found one in Illinois, near Chicago. A proper racing green, with the classic red interior and steering wheel, and the LeMans head fairing, it captivated me immediately. I was particularly taken with the details like 15 inch wire wheels with Dunlop racing tires and aluminum subpanels just like the original cars had.

As a bonus, the right pontoon was signed by two men with Lotus credentials. First, Jay Chamberlain, who drove an Eleven at Sebring, became friends with Colin Chapman, and then became the first importer of Lotus cars for the western USA, and second, Mike Costin who worked at Lotus when the Eleven was the latest and greatest Lotus, and then went on to found a company with Keith Duckworth to build a few race engines. You may have heard of it, it is called Cosworth.

I flew to Chicago, took a rental car to the seller's home and within 30 minutes, bought the smallest, lightest and most open car one could legally drive in this country. Now, anyone with any sense that lived more than 50 miles away would have the car shipped, fettle it carefully, and take a few exploratory trips near home base with friends alerted for the cell phone call which might come at any moment. Not me! Whether this means I have no sense or a need for adventure bordering on that of a human cannonball, I am not quite sure.

The drivetrain for the Westfield is basic Austin Healey Sprite stuff, so it is simple, proven and inexpensive. This gave me the confidence to take the plunge and drive it to Colorado. It had no A/C, no radio or CD player, no seat adjustment, no dome light...I mean, it had no dome!! Not to mention no wipers, no windows, no doors. No problem. To get into the cockpit, for that is what it is, one must climb over a flap that has part of the cockpit surround and part of the windscreen, then fasten it back with a latch and clip. No kidding!

Now, to get it home to Denver, I only had a mere 1,100 easy miles across some of the most scenic, fun, winding, lightly travelled roads in the USA. Or, said another way, what are Illinois, Iowa, Nebraska and eastern Colorado especially *not* noted for... the most scenic, fun, winding, lightly travelled roads in the USA. In fact, I-80 is reported to carry the most truck traffic of all I roads. So, one bright morning, after returning the rental car, I strapped myself into the Westfield Eleven and headed west on US 30 toward home.

At first it was fun. It was a perfect Midwest fall day; warm but not hot, and low humidity. With fall foliage bursting with reds, oranges, yellows and browns, the little green car must have felt at home. Though a bit darty, due to very quick steering and uneven road crown, the ride was remarkably comfortable. The small windscreen did quite a good job of deflecting the wind. Note, however, it is not called a bug screen. Ah, I then remembered why motorcyclists don't smile…it keeps the bugs out of their teeth. Across western Illinois the trip was a delight and I cruised about 65 mph on a good two lane road with light traffic. The Eleven seemed to settle into a nice rhythm with a fine but not too loud rasp from the off side motorbike muffler. We were partners the Eleven and I.

After crossing the Mississippi into Clinton, Iowa the Eleven needed gas and I needed to stretch and find food. I pulled into a place with both. As I untangled myself from the car (remember the alleged door described before?) I turned to face a police cruiser (Picture Luke Skywalker with his X wing fighter facing Lord Vader with the Death Star) and, Vader, I mean the Officer, said to me "That car can't be legal!! License and registration!" Of course, I had no registration in my name, so I gave him the title signed over to me, my license, insurance binder and bill of sale, and waited. After a few minutes and some checking with HQ for a stolen car BOLO, he came back with a wry smile and asked "How far are you going in that thing?" When I answered Denver, he burst out laughing. We talked a while, he returned my documents and then, shaking his head while rolling his eyes in that distinctive manner that says you are the craziest of the crazy, he said "Drive safely in that little space ship!"

I made it well past Des Moines, (which I'm told in English is The Moines) and found a rural motel/cafe to stop for the night. I was quite worn out and fell into a deep carefree sleep. Up at 6:30, I enjoyed a tasty "Home Cooked" breakfast while far from home and hit the road. In order to head west on US 30, I needed to cross the east bound lane then turn west and both lanes had a fair amount of traffic. Now, the ex-Sprite engine was pretty lethargic unless revved and the transmission had a very tall first gear. While that was not a real problem in routine starts, for this blast into a traffic gap in a very vulnerable car, I was in "race start" mode - Lots of revs, slip the clutch and be gone in a flash. What I actually did was start in third gear. Though I realized my mistake right away, I had determined that the extra clutch slip was preferable to being squashed like a bug by a Peterbilt. I made it into the traffic flow, but at the expense of a burned clutch that would not release. Perfect!

I was 700 miles from home in a tiny, open car with a non-functioning clutch. That was no problem once I got rolling; but how was I to get started? I have had to do that sort of thing before so I know that the car will move on the starter in first gear, then fire and pull away. Then matching revs to shift is not too big a deal. There are two big things that impact this scenario though… traffic and stops. Thus, as I rolled west on a two lane farm road through western Iowa, I formulated "the new plan". To avoid both traffic and stops take Interstate 80! By carefully watching my mileage I knew about when I had to stop for fuel and I would watch for a place that I could coast into and start out of on a downhill slope. I found that I could be safe at 150 miles per tank, with a bit of a reserve in the generous five gallon tank onboard. I would watch for a rest stop or easy exit starting at about 130 miles from my last fill and stop there. For two more stops it worked perfectly.

On the Interstate it seemed prudent to move with the flow of traffic which was running about 75 rather than the 65 I had been doing on the two lane road. I had packed a helmet which I hadn't felt I needed, until now, so I put it on and it made a world of difference. It was quiet, bug free and serene at even 80 miles an hour. The little Westfield found a sweet spot at about 77 and I really thought I was going to make it all the way home for the first time in a while. As I rolled along in the right lane, people would start to pass in the left lane and just as they were alongside, the pass would cease and the stares would start. Fingers would point, especially kids in the back seat, smiles would bloom and then the driver would figure that was enough and accelerate on by. After a while I got used to this steady rhythm; passing, pausing, surging on. The exceptions to this pattern were the big trucks.

The 18 wheelers had a purpose and didn't really care about this little green bug darting along in the right lane. That is why when the big tanker truck was almost by and then slowed down and eased back until the cab was alongside me, I looked up to see why. As I turned my head up and to the left, I caught a brief glimpse of a woman in the right seat of the cab and then came the blinding flash. Having captured my "deer in the headlights" look, they seemed satisfied to accelerate away as I tried to keep within my lane and avoid the whirling blue dots. I surely would like a copy of that photo.

We rolled along, the Westfield and I, making good time and without mishap. As I passed Paxton, I looked at the mileage and it was right at 130, so I was planning on stopping at Ogallala 19 miles to the west where there were more services. Right on schedule the exit appeared and as I eased up on the throttle up the ramp the engine stumbled and then died. I coasted as far up the ramp as I could and pulled off to the right side of the ramp in a safe place. The gas station was on the southwest corner of this junction so I started walking the half mile or so up the ramp and over the freeway it would take to get there, buy a can bring it back and start off again to fill up. Actually I was thinking this was good to have a spare gallon or so as the services between Ogallala and Denver are pretty sparse. The walk required a Coke break so it was a while before I got back to the car waiting on the ramp. When I returned and emptied the fuel into the tank I got my next surprise. After 5 or 6 starts in first gear, the starter had packed it in.

I could bump start the car if I had a clutch, but I had none. I could start in gear if I had a starter but I didn't have one of those either. I was still there considering my options when a police car pulled up, lights flashing.

Believe it or not the cop was sympathetic to my plight and suggested we push the car up the exit ramp and over the bridge to the service station complex where it would be safe. He had a padded front bumper that we draped a folded blanket over and gingerly pushed the tiny Westfield up and over to the parking area at the gas station complex. He wished me luck and said he would check on me after he made his rounds, perhaps an hour or so. I said thanks and goodbye. I then contemplated my options.

First was to find a starter in Ogallala, a town of about 4,930 souls which may have a dozen or so English cars within its population of farmers and merchants. Not a likely prospect. The second was to have a starter shipped in from Denver a little over 200 miles away. But where would I have it shipped, where would I stay, how would I install it with my minimal tool set? Option 3 was to call my friend and mechanic Tom Beauchamp in Colorado Springs and see if he could bring one with some tools. So I did.

Tom couldn't find a starter anywhere among his sources, so he thought the best solution, which we will call Option 4, was to come with a trailer and take the car back to the shop. It was indeed the best solution which became abundantly clear later.

Now I had to wait. Tom said it would take a couple of hours to finish what he had to do before he could leave and then it was about a four or five hour drive from the Springs to Ogallala, NE. So I bought a magazine and read it, went for a walk around the complex, and looked through all the fascinating things that were available in the truck stop store. (More CB radios than I had ever seen, tow straps, tie down ratchets, air fresheners, tapes, C/D's and tchotchkes galore. A veritable treasure trove of kitsch I didn't even know existed.) All these activities used up 20 minutes. So I did them all again. And again. Now I only had another six hours to wait. So, I had a leisurely dinner of the Midwest's finest "Home Cooked" meat and potatoes with plenty of healthy, brown gravy.

After dinner, it started to rain. Not a gentle garden friendly rain either, but a genuine Nebraska thunderstorm. My little Westfield Eleven was parked in the lee of the big canopy over the pump area, but the wind was blowing the rain everywhere including the lee of the big canopy. After an eternity, Tom pulled in out of a black stormy night into the lighted oasis of the gas station. It had taken him an extra hour because of the stormy road conditions. Thankfully, the rain eased as we loaded the wounded car onto the open trailer.

We fueled the Suburban, grabbed snacks, used the bathroom and said goodbye to kindly Ogallala, NE. Tom dropped me and my small travel bag off at my home in a southern suburb of Denver about midnight and drove home to Colorado Springs where he got to bed about 1:30 am. The Eleven waited.

When Tom got into the car, replacing the clutch and starter, he went through a check over of the whole car and found that the left front top "A" arm was nearly broken through. If I had continued it most certainly would have broken before reaching Denver and the wheel would have flopped over on its side. I would have had no steering or brakes and at 75+ miles per hour one can only imagine the result. The metal had not been properly brazed and though it looked OK when I inspected the car, the 900 miles had almost broken it through. Both Tom and I are certain that someone was watching over me that day.

Peter Egan refers to this as the great "Trickster" tradition of Plains Indians lore, wherein some embarrassing and inconvenient incident occurs that prevents a major accident. This made sense of course, as I was in the middle of the Great Plains and a six foot tall, old, white guy in a tiny Westfield would certainly be amusing to the Ogallala Sioux.

An example Peter shared was a Cowboy showing off a new hat and having it blown into a mud puddle. Short term it was a bit embarrassing, but while he went home to fetch another hat he missed an encounter with a deadly enemy.

As he wrote: *"What appeared to be bad luck was, in fact, good luck disguised as a minor inconvenience. The Trickster poked fun at your pride, but was actually looking out for your best interest – a guardian angel with a sense of humor."*

In my case, the embarrassment of having a cop push my little car and the inconvenience of a boring evening in a lonely Ogallala truck stop was a minor thing compared to the disaster that would have befallen me at over 70 miles per hour. Maybe the Trickster knew this and shorted out my starter at a convenient truck stop.

Sometime later, while at another truck stop browsing the trinkets, Tom found the perfect little magnetic sticker as a gift. I still have it. It said, and I am not making this up:

Never drive faster than your Angel can fly!

The Westfield on track where it belongs

16 THE OFF ROAD LOTUS

As I waxed poetic about having found a shorter, prettier way to get to Aspen from Denver a question came from my wife Ann: "Why can't you just leave well enough alone? I love that drive through Buena Vista."

She had a point. It isn't as if Denver to Aspen is an empty mindless trek across Nebraska or Kansas. There is the fast way on Interstate 70, which if we were talking about anywhere else in the country would be the short pretty way, and there is our usual path to Aspen, the Lotus route Ann loves; US 285 to Buena Vista, north on US 24 to Twin Lakes and then west on CO 82 over scenic two lane Independence Pass, a highway not frequented by 18 wheelers. Using this route, if one is hustling, Aspen is a solid 4 hour drive from Denver. Part of the reason that it takes 4 hours for a 180 mile drive is that the road doesn't *go to* Aspen so much as it wanders about the mountains through the canyons and, by following the streams over the hills, finally manages to find Aspen with a lot of meandering. In other words, perfect Lotus roads all around.

But we were making the trip with twelve friends in my eight Lotus cars, and I was looking for a really memorable route to impress them. As always, with a group of eight cars (not to mention eight older Lotus cars) driven by people from as far away as England and Pennsylvania, the trip takes longer than it would if I were alone, so I was looking for a shorter route to get us there in a lesser time frame. And so I found Weston Pass.

Colorado has numerous named passes that have varying states of maintenance and capacity. For example, I have been over Mosquito Pass in a vehicle, but I would have been far better served by a rented government mule. There were times when we had to get out of the vehicle and walk ahead as guide to avoid sump puncturing rocks or carefully negotiate eroded gashes that required the lowest gear in the lowest range. On the other hand, I never quite know when I have reached the summit of Trout Creek Pass because it's a beautifully maintained highway with a gradual climb over a very broad summit. Speeds never fall below 65 mile per hour.

My question was where Weston Pass fell in the continuum of difficulty. So, I consulted my Colorado Gazetteer with detailed maps with each road from trail to Superhighway carefully color coded as to degree of difficulty. Weston Pass was coded a "minor maintained gravel road", about midway in the hierarchy of roads and "suitable for a passenger car". Well that was promising, so the next step prior to risking an old Lotus was my illustrated and annotated Book of Colorado Passes. Here I found some specific information and saw how other passes I had traversed were graded.

For example, Boreas Pass is another "minor maintained gravel road" but one that had an additional warning. It required "adequate ground clearance". This was one I had recently driven in my BMW sportwagon with limited ground clearance and wide tires and had found no problem there. I drove at a relaxed pace primarily to limit gravel thrown by the wide tires but at no time was it difficult to proceed. Weston was rated as better than Boreas, with photos to document the point. I felt relieved that Weston was a viable option even with low clearance cars. Research done! Time for a trial run.

So on a fine Saturday, off we went in our M100 Elan to take the scenic shortcut to Aspen. The weather was perfect; another in a string of relentless, sunny, blue sky days with a temperature of about 85 degrees and a light breeze. As we like to say "Just another crummy day in paradise". After passing the town of Fairplay, (yes, you can look it up) we began watching for the sign to Weston Pass. There it was about five miles south of town, a fine two lane paved road that passed through meadows as it climbed toward the snowcapped great divide. The road became gravel after about five miles but it was smoothly graded and plenty wide. We slowed to about 45 miles per hour and wound our way upward. At the divide, the summit of Weston Pass, I was delighted with our short cut. The view was spectacular; the little creek running alongside the road was charming, and the flora and fauna very impressive. So we stopped to get a smiling picture of the triumphant Lotus and its driver.

And, so we continued. As we proceeded, the quality of the road we had experienced at the summit and before began worsening. Within a half mile or so, I was picking my way more carefully among the rocks and erosion channels. Another half mile and I was barely crawling. Ann, not so cheerfully, got out looking for the best way through. We talked about turning around at Ann's suggestion but I really thought we were simply working through a rough stretch resulting from a melting snowfield that was eroding a section of the road. Slowly, carefully, I picked my way along following Ann's directions. "More to the right". "Watch that rock by the right wheel". "Be careful of the muddy spot" The last warning came just as the left front wheel dropped into a mud hole the size of a Papa John's giant pizza. In fact, it was just the right size to encapsulate an Elan tire and wheel,.

Since this is a front wheel drive Lotus, it is well and truly stuck!

Now what? We were well and truly stuck!! I pulled the cell phone out of my pocket and found exactly zero bars of signal. I looked up the pass to the place we had come from and saw no one. I looked down the pass where we were going and saw no one. Ann was not happy with me.

As we surveyed the area, I noticed a few timbers of substantial size and convinced Ann that if I could lever the car up a bit and put something solid under the tire, I could reverse enough to get to solid footing and we would be OK. Of course, being the great sport she is, she jumped right in to help by standing on the timber while I reversed...to no avail.

The more we struggled the worse things got. After about 30 minutes of effort, Ann decided to walk down the road to look for help. I said I would stay and keep trying to get something solid under the wheel and I'd pick her up soon. She had been gone for about ten minutes when I thought that maybe having her alone was not such a good idea. So, I abandoned any thought of a heroic solo release of our car from the mud and went to join her.

Within a few minutes of walking, the first vehicle I had seen all day on the pass crawled up behind me. A pleasant couple in a Ford F150 4WD were out exploring and had only just managed to get around my abandoned car. As he approached he rolled down the driver window and said "Not exactly the right machine for this road is it?" I allowed as how he, Captain Obvious, might be right and asked if I could ride down to civilization with them. They put me behind the seats and as we jostled down the ever rougher "road" that was rapidly deteriorating into "goat path" we met a vehicle coming up the pass. With just enough room to squeeze by each other I saw Ann in the other vehicle through the open windows. It turns out she had been picked up by a guy going fishing who happened to be Mayor of the Town of Leadville. I was once again awed at Lotus owners karma who are in **L**ots **O**f **T**rouble, **U**sually **S**olvable only through the kindness of strangers. We consolidated in the Ford truck with the mayor's advice on the man to see in Leadville for recovery towing. Slowly we worked our way down the pass to the US 24 pavement and were soon at the shop of Millennium Towing and Recovery. We thanked our new friends and walked in to find the Jedi Master of Towing and Recovery.

There we met Bob, the owner and grizzled veteran of picking cars off Weston Pass. In fact, he was so experienced that immediately he let us know the "rules". He said without a trace of irony, "I only work on these terms. $250 to leave the shop and $250 per hour or any part of an hour from the time I leave to the time I am back here!" If he could get up there and back in an hour, it would be $500, maybe $750 or more. What choice did we have? Grudgingly we said OK, so Bob immediately asked for my Visa card to hold until we were done "recovering". He was an expert indeed!

Slowly, and I mean slowly, we retraced our steps to the Elan. Bob took much longer to get there than we did getting down and we had walked part of the way. When we finally arrived at the car he spent about 10 minutes looking at the situation and the car, asking about points that were strong enough to pull from and making a plan. Carefully, he placed the truck on a solid area and walked the cable back to the waiting Lotus. Once he had hooked on the back, walked back to the control panel of the tow rig, it took literally 45 seconds to pull the car some twelve feet back out of the hole. He pulled it back far enough to get it to a place to turn around. Calculated on a per foot basis this is expensive.

Bob, the Jedi Master of Recovery, checks the cable and car before the pull.

Bob made sure that I had cleared the rough area and was motive under my own power and then handed my credit card back. But, only after I wrote in my own hand the exact language that he dictated stating that he was released from any and all claims of damage from the recovery. We had spent over an hour and twenty minutes already so I was expecting the worst, but Bob must have had one tiny shred of kindness left in his heart as he only charged me two hours plus the start fee for a $750 total.

So we started back the way we came, back over the summit down the gravel road and as we finally reached the paved road on the other side of the now familiar pass, we sped up. The car started shaking violently. I was immediately certain that Bob had caused major irreparable damage from the pull and was headed back to Leadville with my signed credit payment while I was left with an undrivable car. I came to a stop and examined the wheel area. There was so much dried mud packed into the wheel and strut that the balance had been changed. It was like a sleeping bag in the washer during the spin cycle as it dances out the door.

Finding a stick, I was able to chip enough dried mud away that some semblance of order was restored. Finally, we were back on the highway at comfortable speed. Bob really was a master of recovery, the Elan cleaned up perfectly and after new CV boots has run fine for many thousands of trouble free miles.

As for us and our shortcut, we finally made it to Aspen with a total elapsed time of, wait for it, over ten hours. This is, of course six hours longer than the so called 'long route' that I had attempted to whittle down. It was a time disaster. Not to mention the recovery fee of $750. If that doesn't qualify as salt in the wound, I don't know what does.

A group of fellow LOCO owners had been waiting for us and had become so worried that they were fully three margaritas ahead of us in drowning their concerns. Needless to say, I got quite a razzing that night from those who "know better" about these things. I fully intend to write the map companies and force reprinting of their guides as to the quality of roadway or goat path.

Fortunately, Ann has been quite gracious the past few years and has hardly ever mentioned Ross' Folly, formerly called Weston Pass.

17 THE CROSS COUNTRY ELAN

The best laid plans, according to Robert Burns, often go awry. I had planned my trip (To the 50th anniversary of the introduction of the Elan to be celebrated at LOG 32 in Orlando Florida) down to the last detail. I had test fitted all the things I wanted to take and made sure that they all fit in the boot in waterproof bags or under the tonneau cover so I could make the trip top down all the way. While Ann has been my companion on many of these boondoggles she had a great response when I first showed her my proposed route. She said, "That looks like fun. You can pick me up at the Orlando airport." So, for once, this trip would be solo. Both ways.

The car was ready having had its "placebo" inspection by Ted over at Sports Car Craftsmen. He calls it that because laying on hands makes us feel better whether or not any real healing occurs. I was ready, having cleared my calendar and paid the bills. But the weather was not ready.

On departure day, October 18th 2012, I awoke to a temperature of 29 degrees. Now, the previous several weeks had seen lows dip into the high 30's but nothing below that. So I faced a dilemma; unpack and put on the soft top or bundle up and tough it out. Of course, I chose the latter.

Looking for all the world like Bibendum the Michelin tire man,, except with a hood over my hat and in green rather than white, I kissed Ann goodbye and headed out. For the first ten minutes or so it wasn't too bad. I had generated a fair amount of internal heat scurrying around getting things ready and I was only travelling at about 45 miles per hour on a city arterial so the wind chill hadn't sucked the heat away yet. Then it got colder. And colder. Despite my bundling up, the cold began to soak in to my bones. By the time I had reached Colorado Springs, an hour south, I was stiffening up from the cold. Still I pressed on and by the time I got to Pueblo, another 45 minutes down the road, I was actually starting to feel my extremities again.

Just south of Pueblo, one lane of the dual lane Interstate highway was closed for a bridge repair and as traffic slowed to 45 mph per the posted lower speed, I found myself behind a semi-trailer who was coming to a complete stop. After a few minutes of not moving, I got curious and angled the Elan to the left enough to see around him. About 30 cars were stopped but I couldn't see why. I assumed a flagman of some kind letting construction work block the lane for a bit. So I decided to soak up some sun and have a snack. Ann had thoughtfully packed some grapes, cheese and crackers and apples along with the required Cokes to wash them down and that sounded really good just then. Ten minutes later after a nice snack and feeling warm for the first time all day, I became aware that some cars behind me were cutting across the median to the freeway entrance and going up the down ramp to the frontage road alongside the highway. So I did too.

As I passed the obstruction I saw both lanes blocked for a bridge repair. Making good time down the frontage road, I suddenly saw many of the cars coming at me in the other lane were those I had seen take the ramp before me. Then I knew why. The frontage road was a dead end. Sheepishly I turned around and retraced my tracks to a single lane underpass to the eastern frontage road and south to the next onramp. It still was shorter than waiting for the lane to open.

A few miles later, I saw a sign reading "Gusty Winds May Exist" which made me think that the Colorado Highway Department must have a metaphysicist on staff. Rather than simply writing "Gusty Wind Area" or "Expect Gusty Winds" we were asked by the sign to ponder their very existence. Is it a wind gust if no one feels it? This cerebral bit of contemplation helped me pass a good quarter hour before I just gave up. As the Shadow used to say, and I'm paraphrasing here, "Who knows what existentialism lurks in the hearts of men? Only the Shadow knows."

As for me, I can assure you that as I was passing through the wind gusts *did* exist and they nearly tore my head right off.

Being warmer improved my mood substantially and I began to appreciate the new taller axle ratio I had installed. Cruising at 65 mph used to be the highest speed that felt comfortable and now I could comfortably do 72-73 mph at the same RPM that I used to do 65. The downside became, as previously mentioned, the wind trying to tear my head off. Still, the day was sunny, the car was running smoothly and I was making good time to Raton where I could get off the Interstate and on to a good two lane road. Stopping for gas I found the first leg mileage figure to be about 33. Not bad at all. I got to my first night stopping point, beautiful Dalhart Texas, by about 3:30 pm including the loss of an hour with a change to Central Daylight Time. This was sooner than I had planned due solely to the increased speed from the new axle ratio.

On the Elan.Net site where I posted the trip details, Rob Walker told why he recalled Dalhart, saying it was: "The only place with a steak house I have ever been in that limits you to 2 glasses of wine or 2 beers, with the admonition that they are not a bar." I found the steakhouse and they ARE a bar...the Bar H Steakhouse! They still limit patrons to just two beers although they did have Blue Moon on tap, along with the "justification" that they are trying to balance good times with responsible hosting. In other words we don't want any liability for how much you drink, good sir!

Day two was an easy day except for the wind. There is a nice flow to US 385 especially between Channing and Vega near I-40. The road rises and falls and swings over hills and down through river valleys and induces a nice rhythm that is quite engaging in the Elan. The fact that there are no other vehicles to interrupt the dance is delightful as well. South of I-40 the road gets boring and drills straight south then cants to the southeast right into Lubbock. I got there just about noon as planned and met my friend and college roommate Dr. Dave Midkiff. Off we set in his air conditioned luxury sedan for a visit to the Buddy Holly museum.

I have been a fan of Charles Hardin Holly's music since it was brand new in the late 1950's. It is still some of my favorite stuff and I know the words and tunes to all the songs he performed in his short 28 month arc of fame until the day the music died, February 3, 1959. He was a huge influence on the Beatles, John Lennon once saying "I AM Buddy Holly" and in fact the Beatles name is based on the name of the original group before it was "Buddy Holly and"...The Crickets. That this small town kid far from the centers of pop music could become the megastar he was before he was 22 is simply amazing. Or just genius.

The Buddy Holly story is most impressive and it is told in a fine little museum but the bonus was the other two museums Dave and I went to, the Silent Wings which depicted the glider transports from WW2 as this was their training base, and the Windmill museum which had over a hundred different windmills and their engineering logic. Both were fascinating, plus it gave me lots of time with Dave. We had a delightful lunch and afternoon though we cancelled evening plans as Dave's wife was sick with the flu and I was quite tired from the wind. I must be getting old.

Between Snyder and Sweetwater Texas I must have seen over a thousand of the big three-bladed wind generators or windmills. This is no exaggeration. There are groups of fifty to a hundred of them on ridge after ridge. Dave Midkiff tells me that these things cost a million dollars each when installed and connected to the grid. In that case I saw over a billion dollars' worth of green engineering on real estate barely worth a plugged nickel.

The Elan in West Texas with 14 of the thousand windmills there.

On the approach to Austin after crossing I-40, I found the beginning of the Hill Country. This, along with the Big Bend area, is one of my favorite parts of Texas. The roads wind and dip, the vistas are lovely, vegetation is varied and the towns are each charming with quite different personalities but all with a Texas attitude of independence and bravado. Near the town of Fredericksburg, I saw the famous Hill Top Café owned by bluesman Johnny Nicholas that Ann and I had been to on the Texas 1000 several years ago. It's a converted 1930's era gas station/ general store with a fun atmosphere---old metal signs and pictures all over the walls and EXCELLENT food. I was hot and thirsty so I stopped in for a spell. I got there just as they were closing from lunchtime but they were kind and poured me a Coke and let me visit about my little car and my long trip. If you ever get the chance - stop by, it is really worth a visit.

Just past Fredericksburg, I saw the turnoff road to Luckenbach, TX as memorialized in Willie Nelson's song. So I turned down the winding and narrow road which was a perfect Elan road seven miles long only to find that Luckenbach was closed. A huge biker convention had taken over the "town" which is all of five buildings. The very pleasant gate guard made it clear that unless I had a pass I wasn't going in. At least the road was worth the fifteen mile detour.

On into Austin I drove with my big plan to visit the Circuit of the Americas the next morning where Mario Andretti was to inaugurate the track in a Lotus 79. There were two problems. One was the University of Texas game that was being played that night so EVERY hotel and motel room was taken and at inflated prices too. There was no room at the inn for a thirty mile radius. The second was that I was barred from entry to the track by about 1,000 big burley construction workers one of whom spent a few minutes sympathizing with me while letting me know in no uncertain terms, I would never get in to the track despite my protests that this was a LOTUS just like the one Mario would be driving in the morning. Ingrates! The closest I got was on a hillside road to the southeast of the fence where I took a memorial photo.

The leg to Galveston was nothing but long straight roads, flat terrain and wind. The worst part came in Houston on Highway 6 which on the map looked to be a clean way to get around the "big city" but turned out to be a route past shopping mall after shopping mall with traffic and turn arrow intersections every two blocks, none of which were synchronized. I have often thought the traffic engineer's intent is to maximize the opportunity to shop rather than make traffic flow and now I am certain. The Elan did not like this. While the engine didn't overheat, the gearbox became stiff and third gear was almost impossible to get into until I got some open road to let air flow through the tunnel. I was worried but that was the only mechanical scare of the trip. Once clear of Houston's negative gravitational pull, it was smooth sailing to the coast. Over the bridge onto Galveston Island was literally a breath of fresh sea air.

Galveston is a neat town with a lot of interesting places to visit, yet very vulnerable to a Katrina type storm any given year. I took the DUCK tour which gave me a sense of the different parts of the town and some history and even included a short water portion mainly I think to demonstrate the amphibious nature of the DUCK more than anything we saw from the water. I had some wonderful seafood and sat overlooking the bay watching the sunset, checked the car over and went to bed. Four days on the road and I was beat while the Elan was doing just fine.

On day five I awoke early and set off on the parkway along the sea wall with the sun just rising over the gulf. Traffic was light and so was my spirit as I made my way to the ferry across Galveston Bay. This ferry is operated by the Texas department of transportation as a free service; sort of a link in the highway system if you will, since the trip around the top of the bay would entail almost a hundred mile trip. As I waited at the ferry port, I could tell that this was a working trip for most of the other vehicles as they were purposeful and focused while I was gaping just like the tourist I was. We passed and

The Elan looks so small on the Ferry

were passed by some really big ships as well as a lot of small working boats all of which seemed to traverse the bay without getting in each other's way even though they were moving in all directions everywhere. Amazing.

Once we had crossed the bay there was not much to see. It was flat, featureless and empty and a road as straight and level as a taut string so I sped up. At a small somewhat dilapidated bait/convenience store and gas station, I found a nice older woman who explained why the road on my map that I planned to take east wasn't really there. It seems that one or two hurricanes ago it was washed out and never replaced, the state figuring that it wasn't worth doing since the major traffic volume went north to Port Arthur and Shreveport. So, that's where I went.

The bridge across Sabine Lake, which separates Texas from Louisiana, is immense. It's only about two miles long but it seems it is about 500 feet high. The huge freighters and tankers that pass through require lots of clearance. This is a part of the country most of us take for granted. It displays the gritty working grind that makes the gasoline and goods available in stores across the land. It functions much as the kitchen and storage at our favorite four-star restaurant. While we appreciate the wonderful meal, we don't know how it gets to the table, and are probably better off. From the bridge top one can see the underbelly of the beast.

Onward I went, turning south, along the bay towards the gulf. Finally, eastbound again, I drove for several hours without seeing anything except random houses along the road. No farms, no towns, no crossroads, no collection of people appeared – just random houses. I have no idea where they get food, fuel or interact with others. It felt like "Dances with Wolves" Cajun style. Finally after probably 125 miles, I came to a small town called Abbeville with modern conveniences…it had a McDonald's. Despite my effort to eat locally, a quarter pounder sounded good about then and Wi-Fi sounded even better. I needed to catch up on a couple of business items…and call Ann.

After the lunch break I was back on the road headed toward my planned stop in Morgan City. I was making good time and the sun was still reasonably high in the sky as I passed MC on a divided Highway 90, so I kept going. That was, as Julia Roberts said in Pretty Woman, "A big mistake". Morgan City was my planned gas stop as well as my night stop. Wouldn't you know it, about 25 miles east the car began to stumble and sputter. I finally remembered to look at the gas gauge and, of course, it was pointing *well **below*** the "E". Doh!

I pulled off past the shoulder to the grass just to get far away from the big trucks zooming by and thought about my predicament. I saw an exit ramp about ¾ of a mile east though I had no idea whether there was a gas station there or not. I decided to call 911 and ask for help.

Normally the idea of running out of gas would not constitute an emergency but I had no other immediate option so I threw myself on the mercy of the operator. I said it was not a real emergency because stupidity doesn't come as a flash out of nowhere; it took me years to cultivate. The operator took pity and said she would have a highway patrol car there within 20 minutes. Sure enough here he came with a training cadet riding along no less.

I started to get in the SUV when the officer asked if I had secured my car. I laughed. "It's a Lotus" I said, "It is impossible to secure". He then recommended I bring everything of value with me. Laden down with computer, jackets, hats and drink cooler, I decided to leave the road atlas.

Stuffed into the rear seat behind the glass partition and next to the K9 screen, I really felt like a dirtbag perp, but they got me to a gas station where I bought the only gas can they had, filled it with 2 gallons and rode with them back to the Elan. During the return trip they asked where I planned to spend the night and I mentioned a town ahead on US 90. "Oh no" they averred, "You don't want to stay there. It is not safe." Instead they told me to take a detour north to a town called Thibodaux. Good call! It is a charming little town with a true Louisiana flavor. I had a Po' Boy sandwich at a small family restaurant that was almost, but not quite, as good as the ones Ann makes (she has ancestors from Louisiana). Then I walked along the little creek and watched the locals fishing. It is good to get off the planned route and the beaten path.

The next morning, day six, I had the challenge about which I felt the most apprehension when planning this trip; getting through New Orleans on Interstate 10. There is really no good way to get through New Orleans except I-10 if you don't want to use surface streets with their stop lights and traffic. So, I sucked it up and clung to the right lane holding my breath until I got to Slidell where I pulled off for a well-deserved rest. I had planned to stop at Café du Monde for a beignet but once I got rolling through the light traffic I decided safe progress was more important than the taste of a New Orleans gourmet doughnut. Boy this car feels small around herds of big transport trucks. I was looking at directional signs *under* a tanker truck next to me.

I turned south on LA 607 to join Highway 90 again and got across Bay St. Louis to the beautiful white sand beaches of the Mississippi Gulf Coast. This was the most satisfying part of the trip as I just "motored" along the Gulf Coast parkway at about 45 mile an hour with the sand and gulf to my right and beautiful homes and stores to my left. It was a pleasant 70 degrees and the Elan was quite happy to float along. I think I only hit about 3 or 4 red lights from Bay St. Louis all the way to

Pascagoula. In Alabama I turned to the southeast and through Bayou La Batre of Forrest Gump fame and down to the beautiful Dauphin Island at the southwestern edge of Mobile Bay. Waiting for the ferry, I had a couple of marvelous fish tacos at the little terminal café and simply enjoyed the warm breezes off the gulf. What a delightful difference from the Colorado cold at the start of my trip oh so long ago.

The Mobile Bay ferry is smaller than the Galveston ferry and they charge by the axle. The 22 foot long Freightliner van that dwarfed the Elan paid the same $18 as I did while the motorcycle which also has two axles and is a lot closer to the size of the Elan paid $8. $18 is a fair price for the trip across the bay, but I mentioned this disparity to the fellow collecting the toll and while he agreed with my logic, he still charged me the full amount. Despite being near the front of the waiting line I was made to wait to board the ferry so I was feeling a bit of discrimination I guess. He told me that they held me back because they wanted to get weight on the ferry to lower the approach angle for my little low clearance car. He was patient and talkative. On the other hand, he had nowhere to go, did he?

The east side of the bay has a parkway much like that along the Mississippi gulf, so I give the same grade to the Alabama Gulf Coast and the Orange Coast all the way to Florida. The afternoon was warm but not hot, there was a delightful breeze and the Elan and I felt right at home. I was just puttering along about 40 mph in third gear when I saw a sign for the National Naval Aviation Museum as I approached Pensacola, not to be confused with Pepsi Cola. As Yogi Berra tells us, "When you come to a fork in the road, take it" so I did; right to the flight museum.

What a place. I suspect anyone who likes the mechanical aspect of cars also likes planes. I know I do and this place is amazing. They have examples of planes from the entire history of naval flight from the first skid mounted track off a destroyer through todays latest. From WWII aircraft and a simulated aircraft carrier flight deck, to models of all the aircraft carriers so you can compare the sizes as they grew, helicopters (including Marine One, the presidential helo) to the Blue Angels formation of five real planes hanging from the ceiling of the atrium. There is only one word to describe it - Overload! If you are ever in

Pensacola make sure you visit this fabulous museum. And best of all, admission is free!

I continued on eastward along the coast, crossed Pensacola Bay and began to look for a good seafood place to stop for dinner. I asked a guy in a car next to me at a stoplight and he said "There is only one place to go for great seafood within the next ten miles…Stinky's Fish Camp just ahead in Navarre". "Stinky's Fish Camp. Really?" I said. At that moment the light turned green and he left before I could get an answer. I figured what the heck, Stinky's Fish Camp it is.

It turned out to be a wonderful recommendation as I had as good a fish dinner as I ever have and the décor was that of a cabin in the woods and not the least bit stinky. After dinner, the sun was setting while I looked out over the gulf so I moseyed back to the car to get to the motel before full darkness enveloped me. While the Elan has good headlights, I never like to be out for long after dark as nobody can see me and I cannot see very well anymore either. I found the motel in Ft. Walton Beach and happily discovered I was about fifty miles further than I had planned to be.

On day seven, I did **not** rest. Instead I decided to cut a day off my planned itinerary and get all the way to Orlando that day. Off I sped at the break of dawn, working my way east around the bays and inlets of the Florida panhandle. Finally I bore straight east on Florida Highway 20 to the Bloxham Cutoff road that veers southeast to US 98, the Coastal Highway which I took all the way to Perry. Perry was my intended seventh night stop which I passed through about noon and began zigzagging my way east and south toward Orlando. When I did stop in a small town for lunch, I looked at the map and found I was within three hours of the hotel in Orlando. Yeehaa! Getting close to my destination I began to get impatient with all the traffic on FL 50 also known as Colonial Drive. Lots of stoplights (almost like it was back in Houston) gave me transmission stress again. But before it, or I, could get too hot I got cool with the experience of a classic Florida downpour.

After a few drops that spit out of the sky as a warning, the heavens opened up. It was a deluge. I turned off the arterial into a shopping center parking lot looking for anything that could shelter me from the rain coming down in buckets. Looking left and right I saw nothing of any kind to pull under for shelter. No trees, no bridges, no parking garages - nothing. Then all at once I saw the entrance to a grocery store that had a cantilevered entry cover about forty feet wide sticking about eight feet out from the building. It extended about twenty feet to the right of the exit door so that is where I headed, straight to the building wall.

The Elan didn't quite fit all the way under the overhang...but it was enough!

Several people were standing there at the exit with their shopping carts waiting for the storm to pass so after stopping just shy of the wall I nonchalantly said hello as if this happened daily. Fortunately for me these were car people and they were glad I had gotten the front two thirds of the Elan under cover. As we stood there waiting for the rain to stop, which they assured me it would within ten minutes, they provided me with exactly the directions I needed to get across the swirling turnpike/interstate, overpass, underpass, interchange, spaghetti maze and to International Drive to the hotel.

I would never have found the direct route they provided but would have wound around through afternoon rush traffic for hours getting more and more stressed. Instead I had a delightful non-stress drive to the hotel. I checked in then treated myself to a steak dinner...I'd had enough seafood.

In reviewing the trip, the Elan had needed **zero** repairs and had never missed a beat other than the lack of fuel (operator error) in Louisiana. I added one quart of oil and 69 gallons of gasoline for a 32 mile per gallon average over the 2,227 miles travelled. Other than the transmission stiffness in Texas, the Elan performed flawlessly.

I had driven, as planned, top down all the way. I got so pumped by that fact that I flashed onto the TOTO song *"Rosanna"* mentally modifying the lyrics like this:

> *All I wanna do when I wake up in the morning is start to drive*
> *Elan-a, Elan-a*
> *I never thought that a car like this could ever energize, Elan-a*

> *All I wanna do in the middle of the journey is accelerate*
> *Elan-a, Elan-a*
> *I thought driving only half this far was tempting fate, Elan-a*

> *Not quite a year since I drove to LOG, Elan, Oh yeah*
> *Now it's done and all I can do is blog, how I went*
> *Top Down all the way, Top down all the way, Elan Oh yeah*
> *Top down all the way, top down all the way, Elan Oh yeah*

These lyrics really entered my head on the more direct trip home which I did NOT do top down all the way. Rather, I took Interstate Highways a fair percent of the way with the top up and earplugs in to make it back home in four days. No problems there either.

Meanwhile, back in Florida on Friday, I had to pick up Ann and it was raining. The trouble happened when I *did* put the top up. When I went to pick up Ann at the airport that afternoon, I was on time but her flight was not. While waiting for her delayed flight, the rain storms came through in waves every ten or fifteen minutes and rainwater found its way through a dozen places in the Elam's supposedly weather tight top .

From the corners of the windshield, above the mirror, where the door meets the body, over the tops of the side windows, it was spitting at me randomly. And every time I would block one area with a towel or sponge the wind would find another place unguarded and water would spit at me from there. I may have been no wetter with no top up. Well, maybe I'd be a little wetter but less frustrated. That's why I went top down all the way!

I know it isn't a modern car but the comments I got from people expecting me to break down at every turn sort of amazed me. Have we become so risk averse and fearful of taking old cars on long journeys that my 4,198 mile round trip is some sort of badge of courage? I hope not. The beauty and charm of the USA is not found on the Interstates with the chain services and endless miles of boredom. While one can make time there, one can rarely make a memory there. It is on the roads that William Least Heat Moon called the "Blue Highways" and those Rand McNally shows as the gray roads that you find the charming, offbeat, interesting and memorable roads and places.

What next for the Elan or any of my other silly little cars and me?

Who knows? But this I *do* know.

There *will* be another Road Trip and it *will* be on the Blue Highways!

The author in his race Elan at Watkins Glen International Raceway in NY

ABOUT THE AUTHOR

Ross Robbins is a 'Car Guy" who enjoys the driving more than the repairing or the preparing of the car. He is a recovering homebuilder who decided on the appropriate proportions when he built his own home with an 11 car garage and 2 bedrooms. He lives with his equally car crazy wife Ann in Littleton, Colorado and drives all his cars as often as he can.

Made in the USA
Lexington, KY
08 November 2014